Karen
Rockey

RUMORS

★ *of our* ★

PROGRESS

have been

GREATLY

EXAGGERATED

★ ★ ★

WHY WOMEN'S LIVES AREN'T GETTING ANY EASIER
—*and* HOW WE CAN MAKE REAL PROGRESS
for OURSELVES *and* OUR DAUGHTERS

★ ★ ★

Congresswoman

CAROLYN B. MALONEY

MODERN TIMES

Modern Times is a trademark of Rodale Inc.

Rodale books may be purchased for business or promotional use or for special sales. For information, please write to: Special Markets Department, Rodale Inc., 733 Third Avenue, New York, NY 10017

Printed in the United States of America

Rodale Inc. makes every effort to use acid-free ♾, recycled paper ♻.

Book design by Christopher Rhoads

Library of Congress Cataloging-in-Publication Data

Maloney, Carolyn B.

Rumors of our progress have been greatly exaggerated : why women's lives aren't getting any easier—and how we can make real progress for ourselves and our daughters / Carolyn B. Maloney.

p.   cm.

Includes index.

ISBN-13 978–1–59486–327–1   hardcover

ISBN-10 1–59486–327–X   hardcover

1. Feminism—United States—History—21st century. 2. Women—United States—Social conditions—21st century. I. Title.

HQ1410.M353   2008

305.420973'09051—dc22   2007047012

Distributed to the trade by Macmillan

2   4   6   8   10   9   7   5   3   1   hardcover

I dedicate this book to my daughters,
Virginia Marshall and Christina Paul. May the battles we fight today
enable them and the generations of women to come to live in a country
where gender equality is not just a privilege but a right.

CONTENTS

ACKNOWLEDGMENTS

*"To make a difference is not a matter of accident, a matter of
casual occurrence of the tides. People choose to make a difference."*

—MAYA ANGELOU

Most of all, I want to thank my family, which inspires me and allows me to follow my dreams. In particular, I want to thank my husband, Clifton Maloney, for being there for me on this book, as he is in every facet of my life. His support and advice were, as always, invaluable. My extraordinary daughters, Christina and Virginia, were generous with their opinions and gave me insight into the concerns of their generation. I learn from them every day.

This book would never have been written without the dedication, hard work, and incomparable talent of my coauthor and quintessential like-minded man Bruce Corwin. His wit, wisdom, and thoughtfulness are evident on every page. Why would a man do a book like this? As he puts it, "If you don't think more women should be running the world, you need to go buy a newspaper."

Keely Savoie, a talented journalist and wonderful writer, did a great deal of research, interviewed many of the women profiled in this book, and helped imbue the manuscript with passion and lyricism.

I also had a dynamic duo of terrific researchers, Katherine Minarik and Laura Welch, for whom this book was a second job and a labor of love.

I am very grateful to my editor, Leigh Haber, for placing her faith in this first-time author, guiding me through the process, and helping me shape my ideas. She and her editing team, Daniel Squadron and Shannon Welch, did a magnificent job of sharpening my prose and helping me hone my focus. I also deeply appreciate the diligence, patience, and professionalism of Modern Times' editorial production team—Nancy N. Bailey and Chris Krogermeier—as well as fact checker extraordinaire Steve Schirra and designer Chris Rhoads.

Much of this book is based on interviews I conducted with women who have accomplished extraordinary things. I truly appreciate their time, their amazing wisdom, and their willingness to share their stories and their vision.

Throughout this process, I relied on the advice of dear friends. I particularly want to thank former congresswoman Patricia Schroeder, Kathy Bonk, Shoya Zichy, and Suzanne Christen, who offered their constructive criticism, insight, and guidance. I especially want to thank Carol Ann Rinzler, who offered me her expert opinion at the time I needed it most and helped make this a better book.

I serve with an extraordinary group of men and women in Congress. I appreciate their fellowship, dedication, and desire to make a difference, and I particularly appreciate those who have worked with me to pass legislation that is important to me.

I am fortunate to represent a remarkable district filled with active, intelligent, hardworking, thought-provoking individuals who bring me brilliant ideas for legislation and never hesitate to offer their opinions. And I want to thank my congressional staff who serves them, both in New

York and Washington. No congressional staff is more effective, hardworking, or loyal. Without their dedication and excellence, I could never have built a body of work worthy of publishing in a book.

Ultimately, all of us who fight for women's rights ride on the shoulders of the founders and brightest lights of the women's movement who are no longer with us: Susan B. Anthony, Betty Friedan, Mary McClintock, Lucretia Mott, Elizabeth Cady Stanton, my husband's distant cousin Alice Paul, Bella Abzug, Barbara Seaman, and so many others. Their courage, sacrifice, and devotion have made it incumbent on us all to make their dream of equal rights for women come true.

INTRODUCTION

*"Never doubt that a small group of thoughtful, committed citizens
can change the world; indeed, it's the only thing that ever has."*

—MARGARET MEAD

Until I was 17, I focused much more on ballet than on community service. Then, a terrible accident changed my life. A drunk driver ran a red light, hitting the car I was in. I was thrown to the pavement. My leg lodged in the axle of the other car as it spun around, dragging me with it. When I came to, my head was just inches from a tire. My femur was badly broken; my body was battered from head to toe. I spent the next six months of my 17th year in the hospital in traction, then another six months at home in a body cast.

I can't say I resolved to overcome adversity, take advantage of a second chance, and devote my life to a singular mission. Life is rarely as simple as such story lines go. But when you come within inches of getting killed, you can't help but wonder whether you were spared in order to live a life of consequence. And when you spend six months in a plaster prison, you can't help but empathize with people who endure hardship all their lives.

As of age 17, my ballerina aspirations were history. But a whole new world was about to open up.

In the South in the 1950s and '60s, girls were taught the virtues of modesty and modest ambitions. Good manners were as important as good grades. The only "sport" we could go out for was cheering for boys who played sports. The only economics we studied was home economics.

Often, the girls studied hard while the boys hardly studied, but it didn't matter. Boys were told they could grow up to do whatever they wanted. Girls, including me, were encouraged to be teachers, nurses, librarians, and secretaries (if they weren't already wives and mothers by the time they finished school). The idea that I would someday become a politician in New York City was as inconceivable to me as playing quarterback for the New York Giants.

I didn't rebel against the deferential mind-set of the community I lived in. I was a good girl who got good grades. I was a cheerleader and homecoming queen. I recently found an old photo of me wearing a dress and a sash that said "Miss Hospitality." I tried to remember what the event was, then realized that I didn't want to know.

That car accident was the first step in a gradual process. I went to college and moved to New York. The more I saw, the more I realized that the deferential part I had played in my girlhood hadn't been written for me.

After a few stints in the corporate world, I did what I was encouraged to do as a child: I went into teaching. Wanting to help people who really needed my help, I got a job working with welfare recipients who were trying to get their high school equivalency degrees in East Harlem.

The women I worked with faced terrible decisions every day: diapers or milk, dinner or rent, go deeper into debt or postpone Christmas until next year. Watching them earn their degrees, get jobs, and help their kids with their homework was an amazing experience that hooked me on women's issues and public policy for good. At the micro level, that government program had showed me the tremendous power of government to improve people's lives.

At the macro level, I saw the power government has when it enacted

Title VII to establish equality of opportunity in employment, Title IX to establish equal opportunity in the classroom and on the playing field, and *Roe v. Wade* to enhance women's right for self-determination.

One of the main reasons I am in Congress today is that I wanted to help push progress forward.

As I LOOK AROUND at how American women are doing today, the story is mixed.

Based on some indicators, one might think that women have never been better off. Violence against women is down. Girls and young women are thriving at school. We have a female Speaker of the House and, as of this writing, a woman with a real shot at the presidency.

Yet there are many areas in which women's rights are being eroded and women's vital needs are not being met. The wage gap is narrowing at a snail's pace. Reproductive rights are more restricted than at any time since the *Roe v. Wade* decision in 1973. Sex discrimination complaints, although falling, are higher now than they were in the year after the Clarence Thomas/Anita Hill hearings.[1] The health-care system, which women use more frequently than men, has become so dysfunctional—and its inequities so indecent—that 90 percent of Americans believe it needs either fundamental changes or a complete overhaul.[2] Indecent, regressive changes to the tax code have cut into the social services that women disproportionately utilize, and they are likely to lead to deeper cuts in the future. America's percentage of children enrolled in early education programs that are critical to child development and help enable women to balance work and family is tied with that of Equador—39th in the world.

And while we tell our daughters that women can do anything, we still have not managed to include women in the US Constitution by enacting an equal rights amendment.

Many on the right preach "moral values," but policies like these lack the moral values that matter most. I call them *human* values: fairness, compassion, generosity, tolerance, honesty, humility. Or to sum it up in one word: decency.

Too many government policies contribute to what I call the decency deficit. Abuse of power, greed, corruption, and arrogance collapsing under its own weight contributed strongly to the change of control in Congress in 2006 and the growing perception of the Bush presidency as a failure. But there have been bipartisan failures as well in meeting the needs of women, children, and families, and they have taken their toll.

Studies have shown that women have become less satisfied with their lives over the past 30 years[3] and that there is a growing "happiness gap." Men feel happier with their lives than women do, and the disparity is growing.[4]

It might be because the average woman has lost the equivalent of one night of sleep per week since 1979. Or that women report it's getting harder to balance work and family. Or that meeting the standards of being a good employee, a good mother, and good-looking gets more impossible every day.

It's fair to say that overall, *at best*, women's lives haven't gotten any easier. I believe it's also fair to say that rumors of our progress have been greatly exaggerated.

For every failure in Washington, however, there are thousands of success stories, from Maine to Hawaii. Many milestones have been achieved. The US Women's National Soccer Team sold out the Rose Bowl in Pasadena, California, and Giants Stadium in East Rutherford, New Jersey, during the 1999 World Cup, which they won. Oprah Winfrey has become arguably the most powerful person in media and the first African American female billionaire. Eileen Collins, whom I met on Capitol Hill, became the first woman to command a space shuttle mission.

But even more important, I never cease to be amazed by the courage, resiliency, and accomplishments of so many everyday American women whom I encounter. They grace the many lives they touch, as executives or educators, cops or carpenters, stay-at-home moms or entrepreneurs.

In this book, I will introduce you to amazing women who infuse decency into everything they do and exude human values in a world that badly needs them. One is rape survivor Debbie Smith, who helped me pass a bill that will, by one estimate, put 50,000 rapists behind bars with DNA testing. Another is former student activist and current staffer Linda Forman, whose creative protest helped shame Wal-Mart into stocking emergency contraception. A third is Martha Stewart Living CEO and my neighbor Susan Lyne, who is giving headhunters a list of 100 women who would make great board members.

You will also hear from some women you already know, like Mia Hamm, Meryl Streep, and Pat Schroeder—pioneers who have used their platforms to advance progress for women.

I will explore the eight goals we must accomplish to establish America as the world's most woman-friendly country, pay down the decency deficit, and make women's lives easier. I'll make some suggestions on how you can help. I'll tell you about "everyday activists"—women who got creative about making change in ways both big and small on issues they cared about in their own communities. And I'll point you to some great women's groups that have some great ideas on how you can get involved and make a difference.

I hope to persuade you that *any* action in support of your beliefs matters, whether it is large or small, brief or time-consuming, successful or unsuccessful. I lost so many battles as a member of the minority party in Congress before 2007 that this book could be called *Zen and the Art of Legislative Losing*. But none of those battles were a waste of time. They drained my energy, but they also filled my heart and built support for future victories.

Despite what the book's title implies about where we are at present, I'm very optimistic about the future of women and girls. I am thrilled by the confidence of the next generation. Far more so than when I was growing up, women and girls have opportunities to apply their talent, education, skills, and decency to make America the world's most woman-friendly country.

Over time, if we all strive to make a difference both inside and outside Washington's Beltway—as workers and moms, scholars and senators, mentors and coaches, activists in religious congregations and community organizations—American women will prove once again that we are as unstoppable as we are incomparable. We can be the business leaders who create jobs for women and maintain America's economic preeminence. We can change the attitudes of the workforce and government to foster *real* family values, creating a saner work/life balance for all parents, married or single. We can end violence against women by more effectively prosecuting its perpetrators and protecting its victims. We can create a health-care system that puts people ahead of profits. We can restore the decency and human values on which this country was founded. We can change the rules. We can change the world.

And I expect we will, because the power of women, when we resolve to do something, is one thing that can never be exaggerated.

THIS BOOK IS BASED on the single core belief that we really can make a difference.

You don't have to become a full-time public servant to make an impact. I see women and men making a difference every day in so many ways: by getting involved in local politics; acting as positive role models in their families, companies, schools, and towns; organizing like-minded people to address issues or rally around specific causes; becoming "everyday activists" and changing things at a grassroots level.

It may seem overwhelming to think about all the progress we have yet to make and all the issues there are to address in our nation and world. And it may seem intimidating or even downright scary to take on large and sometimes very ugly problems. But if we all do *something*, things really can change.

I've felt discouraged or intimidated many times in my life and career. One of my greatest inspirations for pushing ahead is advice that was passed along by my father. He spoke at my sister's high school graduation as I sat in the audience, recovering in a full body cast from my near-fatal auto accident. Those were dark days for me, and I wondered if my life was ever going to get back on track. His words about the future inspired me, and again and again, I still go back for inspiration to the words of the 18th-century German writer Johann Wolfgang von Goethe that he shared that day:

> Until one is committed, there is hesitancy, the chance to draw back. Concerning all acts of initiative (and creation), there is one elementary truth, the ignorance of which kills countless ideas and splendid plans: that the moment one definitely commits oneself, then Providence moves too.
>
> All sorts of things occur to help one that would never otherwise have occurred. A whole stream of events issues from the decision, raising in one's favor all manner of unforeseen incidents and meetings and material assistance, which no man could have dreamed would have come his way. Whatever you can do, or dream you can do, begin it. Boldness has genius, power, and magic in it. Begin it now.

That quote inspired me again as I was running for my first term in Congress in 1992. The race was incredibly tough. I was running against a

14-year Republican incumbent who would outspend me 5 to 1. Everywhere I turned, people told me that I was going to lose. Few people would donate money to run my campaign because they didn't think I could win. It was very discouraging.

But one day during the race, I sat down to work at a local coffee shop. I looked up and, miraculously, there on the wall was the quote my father had shared all those years before.

I urge you to remember those words, or at least the spirit of them. If you care about doing something, changing something, make that commitment, and good things will happen. If you are a longtime activist, redouble your commitment. Your service *will* make a difference, both in the world and in your heart.

If you're not sure where to begin, pick just one thing that you feel passionate about. Do one bold thing for another woman or girl.

Boldness has genius, power, and magic in it. Begin it now.

1

A WORKPLACE THAT WORKS
FOR FAMILIES

"No one can make you feel inferior without your consent."

—ELEANOR ROOSEVELT

t shows up in all the statistics, but we rarely see it as it is happening. Still, the results are visible all around us—more men than women at executive meetings, few women in hard hats at construction sites, more male floor managers and more women cashiers. Too often, we don't dwell on it. We watch television shows and see an equal balance of male and female detectives, surgeons, and lawyers. We take comfort in the thought that life must be imitating art—maybe not in *our* community, but surely somewhere close by.

Every now and then, though, each of us gets a stark, jolting glimpse of discrimination against women in all its raw ugliness—discrimination that continues to seep unchallenged into the very fabric of American life. At these moments, we know in our hearts that the statistics are true, that the problems persist.

I was first elected to Congress after the women's movement had battled for three decades to secure hard-won rights for women in the workforce. Major civil rights victories for women in the workplace had been scored while I was still a teenager. The Equal Pay Act of 1963 established as law the principle of "equal pay for equal work." In 1964, Title VII of the Civil Rights Act made it illegal to discriminate on the basis of sex, race, color, religion, or national origin. In 1967, President Lyndon B. Johnson issued an executive order that extended affirmative action requirements to the hiring of women as well as minorities. In 1972, Title IX guaranteed women equal access to education (including extracurricular activities), leading to a huge increase in women college graduates entering law, medicine, and nontraditional fields of study and work. In the 1970s, "women need not apply" job descriptions fell by the wayside, and women were finally able to get credit in their own names. In 1978, the Pregnancy Discrimination Act barred employers from firing, refusing to hire, and not promoting women because of pregnancy or related conditions.

By the end of the 1980s, it was no longer a novelty (although it was and still is a rarity) to see women construction workers standing on the beams of hotels as they were being built in addition to making the beds after the hotels opened, welding cars on factory floors as well as taking dictation, and working in the cockpits of commercial airplanes as well as in the cabins.

These advances, along with major shifts in cultural attitudes, brought women in the workforce substantial advances that enriched our lives, enhanced our self-esteem, created strong new role models for our daughters, and made our society more equitable, productive, and dynamic.

But all is not well.

In the mid- to late 1990s, as glossy magazines churned out cheerful stories about flexible, family-friendly workplaces, anecdotally, I wasn't seeing it. Women kept telling me that their employers were demanding more and more. Working mothers seemed to be having the hardest time.

They were being passed over for promotions, marginalized if they asked for a flexible or part-time schedule, and fired first in the growing number of downsizings.

I was also hearing stories about pressure being put on employees to work longer, less family-friendly hours. Globalization requires companies to compete around the clock, so employees increasingly are asked to be available around the clock.

The workplace seemed to be placing more and more value on "ideal workers," a phrase coined by Joan Williams, professor of law and director of the Center for WorkLife Law at the University of California Hastings College of the Law in San Francisco. "Ideal workers" are employees who are unconstrained by outside responsibilities, including family. By definition, mothers suffer the most in the face of the ideal worker standard, which negatively judges those who have caregiving responsibilities.

By 2000, my instincts were telling me that the workplace actually *wasn't* becoming more family friendly and that women no longer seemed to be making steady gains in workplace equality. I wanted to try to quantify this phenomenon, if there indeed was a phenomenon to quantify. I hoped I was just being paranoid.

So Representative John Dingell (D-MI) and I requested of the nonpartisan Government Accountability Office (GAO) a study on the wage gap. Unfortunately, the initial GAO study proved my paranoia to be fact and confirmed my worst fears.

• In 7 of 10 industries that employ more than 70 percent of women workers and managers, the wage gap between men and women managers actually grew between 1995 and 2000.[1] Further, women held a share of management jobs proportionate to their share of the industry workforce in only 5 of the 10 industries.

- Being a parent held women back.
  - After couples had children, fathers' incomes went north and mothers' incomes went south.[2]
  - Sixty percent of male managers had children, compared to just 40 percent of female managers.[3]

Clearly, something was wrong, and we wanted more information.

So Representative Dingell and I requested a second, more comprehensive study to offer insight into the sources of the wage gap.

The second study reviewed nearly 20 years of data on workers at all levels, not just managers. It controlled for demographic and work-related factors such as occupation, industry, race, marital status, and job tenure. It also controlled for work patterns: the fact that women on the whole have fewer years of work experience, work fewer hours per year, are less likely to work full-time, and leave the labor force for longer periods than men do. These are many of the factors cited by wage-gap defenders who claim it can be explained by women's freely made career choices.

The report's conclusions were unequivocal. "Even after accounting for key factors that affect earnings," its authors said, "our model could not explain all of the difference in earnings between men and women."[4] The study suggested that discrimination could account for at least part of the discrepancy.

Bad news, but hardly surprising.

But I was also concerned about some of the things the study's design *did* control for. *Why* do women have fewer years of work experience, work fewer hours per year, tend to be less likely to work full-time, leave the labor force for longer periods, and work in lower-paying professions? Are those "choices" really freely made, or are they dictated by the constraints of inflexible workplaces, discrimination, and stereotypes about what "women's work" entails?

Over the past several years, I've read a great deal of the related research and had many conversations with women and men in the private sector in an effort to understand why women aren't getting ahead. I've concluded that while some mothers cheerfully flatten or invert their career trajectories to raise children, there are serious flaws in the workplace and in public policy. More often than not, it is these flaws, rather than an enthusiastic choice, that force mothers out of the workforce.

In the American workplace, equality is still out of reach, as these statistics show.

- Women managers made 79.7 cents to a man's dollar in 2000—0.7 percent *less* than they made in 1983.[5]

- In 2000, 70 percent of respondents said earning enough to pay their bills and spend time with their family was getting harder, not easier.[6]

- The US Census Bureau reported that the percentage of women in executive management positions actually fell from 32 percent in 1990 to 19 percent in 2000.[7]

MORE LEAVE, MORE RETURNS

When I got the news in 1980 that I was pregnant with my first child, my first reaction was joy that I was about to become a mother. My second reaction was fear that my career might never be the same. There were two major questions: Should I quit my job to take care of my child full-time, and would my employer give me any choice?

I decided to try to hang on to my job because it was as hard earned as it was improbable. As I noted in the introduction, in the traditional South where I was raised, the role models for girls were teachers, nurses, librarians, secretaries, and homemakers. All of these are worthy, even wonderful choices, but back then, they were virtually the only ones. When I was growing up, I assumed I would make one of those choices.

After graduating from Greensboro College in North Carolina in 1968, however, I visited a friend in New York. I fell in love with the city and traded a genteel life in the South for the buzz of the Big Apple. The first job I had a passion for was, in fact, a teaching job: helping welfare recipients in East Harlem pass the high school equivalency exam. When funding for my employer was put on the chopping block, I became deeply involved in lobbying to save it. During that ultimately successful campaign, I realized that as a teacher I could help 20 to 30 students improve their lives, but working in public policy would allow me to help thousands of people.

First I took a job with the New York City Board of Education, then moved to the New York State Assembly, and then joined the office of

Have you ever seen a cowboy movie set in Massachusetts? Neither have I. There simply aren't many cowboys in the native habitat of Senator Edward Kennedy. But that didn't stop the Massachusetts State Police from requiring women to be proficient cowgirls if they wanted to maintain their duties during a pregnancy.

Caryl Sprague, Lisa Butner, Susan Howe, Sarah O'Leary, and Brenda Watts were all veteran Massachusetts state troopers who became pregnant during the same year. Four of them had worked during previous pregnancies and had stayed on the job until delivery without restriction of their activities.

This time was different. A new Massachusetts State Police policy required that unless a state police surgeon certified that

Democrat Manfred Ohrenstein, the minority leader of the New York State Senate.

I was Senator Ohrenstein's director of special projects when I became pregnant. Although Senator Ohrenstein was a strong advocate for women's issues, most employers at the time took it for granted that a woman would leave her job when she had a baby. But I wanted to go back to work after I had my baby.

I told Senator Ohrenstein that I was pregnant—and that I wanted to return to my job after having the baby. I just happened to mention this at a party I was giving in his honor.

He was very polite but incredulous that I would think of returning. The State Senate's human resources representative wasn't even polite when I called to ask what kind of leave was offered for pregnancy.

"Leave? What kind of leave?" the woman asked. "Most women just

the women could safely complete specific tasks, they would be put on restricted duty. Then, they could have no contact with the public and would be forbidden to wear their uniforms, drive their assigned cruisers, and work overtime.

The so-called essential tasks included shoveling snow, mowing lawns, and roping large animals off roads—so I dubbed it the "cowgirl standard."

Inevitably, all five were put on restricted duty.

They filed complaints with the Equal Employment Opportunity Commission, and eventually, justice was served. An appeals court ordered the Massachusetts State Police to pay four of the women $1 million total in punitive damages[8] and called the episode an "unprofessional charade." Brenda Watts was denied compensation on technical grounds.[9]

leave." She told me that a pregnant woman had never asked to keep her job. She suggested I apply for disability and see what happened. I rejected that idea on principle because pregnancy isn't a disability, it's a joyous event.

I realized I was going to have to get creative.

Political offices are themselves very political, and others were lobbying to take over my job. I didn't want another staff member to fill my position when I went on leave, lest he or she want to keep it when it was time for me to return. So I asked my friend Suzanne Christen to fill in for me.

Senator Ohrenstein was supportive and kept my job available for me.

But after combating the pressure to quit at work, I started being similarly pressured by my husband, Clif. He calculated that with the cost of taxes, child care, and other expenses that accrued with my working outside the home, my job would be a net loss. Our family would be better off financially if I were a stay-at-home mom!

I couldn't argue with the numbers. I could only argue with my husband about what to do next. I didn't want to quit my job. I *loved* it. But I loved my husband, too—and the idea of being a mom. So I was torn.

Then I went for a walk in Central Park with civic leader Eleanor Guggenheimer. She was a veritable lioness in New York City politics, and I was proud to call her a mentor. If you were a young Democratic woman working in government, when Eleanor talked, you listened.

"Don't do it," Eleanor told me. "Hold on to your job. If you continue working, you'll continue advancing. If you leave now, you're going to limit your options. It's going to be hard for you to get back to the level where you are now. As much as you love your daughter and want to be with her all the time, she will grow up and leave you. She will go off and live her life, and you'll be left without a career. And what if your husband leaves you? Where will you be then?"

I was sold. Telling Clif my decision was tough, but soon he not only embraced my choice, he became the most ardent supporter of my career as an elected official.

Ultimately, Eleanor was right. My husband never left me, but Christina grew up and moved out, as children do. She graduated from the New York University School of Law, is working for a law firm, and has her own apartment in New York City.

Making the decision not to leave the workforce—despite the fact that my job was costing us money—proved over time to be professionally and financially rewarding. Many of my friends yielded to the conventions and constraints of the times and grudgingly left the workforce to have children. As Eleanor had predicted, the careers of most never fully recovered.

Because of this experience of wanting to have both children and a career, as a member of Congress I supported the Family and Medical Leave Act (FMLA) of 1993 with great personal satisfaction. It was the first major federal bill that tried to balance work and life for Americans. It guaranteed a majority of American workers[10] 12 weeks of unpaid leave to care for a newborn or newly adopted child or a sick relative or to recover from a serious illness. Congress had passed the FMLA seven times, but presidents Ronald Reagan and George H. W. Bush had vetoed it every time. President Bill Clinton signed it into law.

I felt pretty good about it. Yes, the leave was unpaid, but I expected additional federal-level measures on work/life balance to eventually be passed, including paid leave, which would make women's lives easier and help working families.

My expectations were wrong. Some Republicans in Congress and the Bush administration have not only stopped progress in its tracks but have also flirted with reversing it.

The US Chamber of Commerce and other groups testified before Republican-controlled Congressional subcommittees and held closed-door meetings with Labor Department officials. The chamber's head of labor policy called changing the FMLA its "number one priority right now in terms of labor issues." One of the groups lobbying for change along with the chamber is a cadre of companies, organizations, and associations that cynically calls itself the National Coalition to Protect Family Leave.

The coalition has been advocating a change in regulation of the FMLA that would allow employers to wait an additional eight *business* days before notifying employees whether their leave is FMLA protected.[11] They say that they merely want to implement regulations "to ensure that the application of the law is consistent with congressional intent." But, in the words of attorney Lawrence Lorber, who represents and counsels companies on employment and labor law, "one person's reform is another person's gutting."

I can't speak for the entire Congress, but *my* intention was to pass a law that would allow workers and their families to respond to life-altering and life-threatening situations without losing their jobs. My intent was to allow workers and their families to offer love and support to one another in challenging moments without risking destitution. Those are *my* family values, and don't let anyone tell you that Democrats don't have them. Since control of Congress changed in 2006, it is unlikely the chamber and the coalition will succeed in advancing legislation that would roll back FMLA. Unfortunately, no legislation needs to be passed to weaken the FMLA. It can be done by the Labor Department's decree. In early 2007, the DOL issued a request for public comment on the FMLA, a potential precursor to gutting it.

I've introduced two bills to strengthen it. One bill would, among other things, allow employees to take their kids to the doctor for routine visits and visit their schools to meet with their teachers. The second bill would apply the FMLA to a larger circle of close relatives and to lesbian and gay domestic partners.

Senator Edward Kennedy (D-MA) and I also have introduced legislation that would help workers pursue reduced or modified work hours so they can better meet family obligations. Modeled after successful legislation adopted in Great Britain, our bill, the Working Families Flexibility Act, would give employees a right to request modification of their work hours, would provide job protection for employees who make such requests, and would require employers to provide an explanation for requests that are denied.

I hope that the election of 2006 marked the beginning of a new era, one in which we begin to equalize the balance of power between ordinary working families and special interest groups. But I also know that to truly embark upon a new era, women and families across the country who care about these issues must get involved and fight for *their* family values.

THE MATERNAL WALL

In 1999, Dawn Gallina was a new associate in the Reston, Virginia, office of the Boston law firm Mintz, Levin, Cohn, Ferris, Glovsky, and Popeo. For several weeks, the job seemed to be going well.

Then, Dawn says, everything changed when a managing partner learned that she had a young child. The partner expressed dismay and admonished her for not revealing her motherhood during her interview. From then on, he frequently made demeaning comments about Dawn and her work.

But the problem at the firm wasn't limited to the partner. Another partner soon let slip what I call a Revealing Act of Candor (RAOC)—

something that many people may think but usually have the good judgment not to say. He told Dawn that she had to decide whether she wanted to be "a successful mommy or a successful lawyer" and disparaged the work of female attorneys in general.

When Dawn complained to the firm's headquarters in Boston, she was asked not to file a formal complaint. She was assured that the firm would take care of the problem.

Shortly thereafter, Dawn was told that her complaint had "embarrassed" their office. Then both men began to actively retaliate against her.

Dawn says she sought support from female colleagues who had had similar experiences, but the advice of the head of Mintz Levin's human resources department was to "keep [your] head down and do [your] work."

One day, Dawn had to leave the office for a medical emergency involving her daughter. When she had a chance to check her voicemail later on, she had a message informing her that she had been terminated for "poor performance."

Dawn filed suit for gender discrimination, retaliation, and sexual harassment. The retaliatory discharge complaint went to trial, and the jury ruled in Dawn's favor. Mintz Levin appealed, but Dawn won again, and the firm settled for a substantial sum.

Still, the male partners kept their jobs, while Dawn eventually took an in-house counsel job at a corporation in Richmond.

"I have not worked for a law firm since, and I would consider myself completely tainted by the experience [if I did]," she explained in 2005 to Kris Hundley of the *St. Petersburg Times*. "Though the Washington, D.C., area is large, the legal community is very insular."

She continued, "You have to ask yourself, 'Do you want to remain in an organization that condones that kind of behavior, or do you want to speak out?' And if we don't say anything, it's not going to get better."[12]

In her book *Unbending Gender,* Joan Williams says that cases like

The maternal wall is not imaginary. Its existence has been proven time and again.

One study[13] identified a subconscious stereotype in the workplace: When women give birth, they are viewed by their colleagues as kinder and gentler—and less capable. Their "warmth" ratings go up, but their "competence" ratings go down. When men have children, their warmth ratings go up, but their competence is perceived to remain unchanged. A high competence rating increases your chances of being hired and promoted. A high warmth rating makes you more likely to be smiled at in the hallway, but it won't help you get equal pay.

Dawn's embody what she has dubbed the "maternal wall." The maternal wall is constructed of the mounting demands of the "ideal worker" standard and other discrimination, conscious and otherwise, against mothers. Dawn ran headlong into a common stereotype connected with the maternal wall: that mothers aren't committed enough to their jobs to succeed.

WORK *AND* LIFE

Some companies are encouraging women and men to take greater advantage of the work/life balance policies on their books. One of them, the Big Four global accounting firm KPMG, is doing a lot for families. New mothers get six months of maternity leave, and KPMG is open-minded about nontraditional work arrangements.

The experience of Manal Corwin, sister-in-law of my coauthor on this book, Bruce Corwin, illustrates KPMG's flexibility. In 2004, Manal, the mother of three children ages 10, 8, and 3, decided she needed to devote more time to her kids. She'd served successfully for 13 years in law and

Studies show that men *are spending more time with their children and sharing caregiving responsibilities more than they used to and that having both parents involved in children's lives is enormously important. For example, to accommodate my grueling work schedule, Clif is a supportive and wonderful father who has done a lot of the work of raising our daughters, and his involvement undoubtedly has played a huge role in helping them become bright, confident women who are ready to take on the world.*

Some companies are encouraging men to take greater advantage of their work/life balance policies. KPMG's late chief executive officer Eugene O'Kelly strongly emphasized during his tenure that men should take two weeks of paternity leave. At KPMG, the number of eligible men taking paternity leave rose from less than 20 percent in 2000 to more than 80 percent in 2004.

But more men than women view work/life balance programs, especially part-time work or job sharing, as illegitimate in their work environments.[14] As a result, men generally settle for the all-or-nothing employment model, usually opting for "all" by remaining employed full-time. Work/life balance programs become as gender-neutral in practice as they are on paper.

I like to say that there will never be equality for women until there is equality for men.

government, culminating in her appointment as a principal at KPMG's National Tax Office.

When she told her managers she was leaving, they urged her to propose a part-time schedule and compensation package that would work for her family and the company.

"After that conversation, I was pretty confused!" Manal says. "It was a difficult decision, but I had pretty much decided that I wanted to move on and deal with a new phase of my life. I was excited about it. Suddenly, I had a whole new dilemma on my hands. But they were asking me to write my own ticket, which was a great option to have."

She got comfortable with the idea of working 20 to 25 hours a week, but only with an arrangement under which she would not be marginalized if she did. In the end, Manal agreed to stay on part-time. She telecommutes some days, travels occasionally, and participates in essential client matters. She says she continues to do interesting work, hasn't "lost relevancy," and feels that many of her colleagues—most of whom are men—embrace her role.

The new arrangement has been rewarding for her family, allowing her to help with homework after school, participate in school activities, and spend more quality time with her kids.

Family-friendly policies that keep workers engaged and employed are good for the bottom line. KPMG estimates that a resignation costs the company one to one and a half times the former employee's salary. Between 2003 and 2007, the number of women leaving the firm fell by 20 percent. That adds up to a lot of savings.

Higher retention means more promotions. In 2000, just 7.5 percent of partners were women. By 2008, that number exceeded 18 percent, highest among the Big Four.

"All of which leads us to believe that the programs we have put in place are actually taking hold," says Joseph Maiorano, KPMG's executive director of human resources. It certainly seems that way.

Unfortunately, despite the economic advantages of an enlightened policy, KPMG may be the exception to the rule.

• On average, companies with the highest percentages of women board directors have a 53 percent higher return on equity than those with the least.[15]

• Businesses with family-friendly benefits experience higher productivity and lower absenteeism and attrition.[16]

• The number of women corporate officers at Fortune 500 companies barely budged between 2002 and 2005, rising a mere 0.7 percent to 16.4 percent.[17]

• Women of color held just 1.7 percent of corporate officer positions and were only 1 percent of Fortune 500 top earners.[18]

• Eighty-five percent of respondents reported that their company offered no maternity or paternity leave benefits.[19]

CHILD-CARE CARING?

I recently read about a company at which 500 women workers who were subject to mandatory overtime and shift extensions had their babysitters drop off their children at the workplace. They told the aghast managers and security guards that because they would be put in prison and their children would be taken away from them if they left them home alone, the children had to stay there since the women had to stay at work. (Job security alert: Don't try this without a union card.)[20]

At least those women had their union to protect them. Corporations are increasingly hiring subcontractors and temporary workers or "leasing" employees (essentially, employing long-term temps).

At all levels of the labor market, I can see that the workplace isn't working for millions of American families. As a federal official, I'm deeply troubled by our government's unconscionable disregard for the needs of the children of working families.

Many mothers, especially those who are single, can't afford not to work full-time, so they must find other options for caregiving. This might be all right if quality child care were affordable or available. But it isn't.

Only 10 percent of child-care centers in the United States meet the standards of the nation's leading child-care watchdog group.[21] This problem stems in large part from America's failure to create a national child-care system for families other than the poor or near-poor who qualify for the few underfunded programs that do exist.

Dorothy Conniff, who, as community services director for the city of Madison, Wisconsin, increased the city's number of accredited child-care programs from 9 to more than 80, says there are consequences to leaving millions of infants and toddlers languishing in child-care centers of dubious quality. "There are windows of development for key abilities during the first three to five years of life, before a child ever starts public school," she says, "where their language capacity, problem-solving skills, and much of their social skill [set] are on a path that's extremely difficult to change. It's tragic. The kids that are left that far behind are never going to find the kind of employment that will lift them out of poverty."

In 2007, I invited Nobel Laureate James J. Heckman to testify before the Joint Economic Committee to discuss his research, which shows that for every dollar invested in early education, $17 is returned to society. That's why I introduced the Prepare All Kids Act of 2007 with Senator Robert Casey (D-PA) to help states expand their pre-K programs and child-care services. Early interventions promote higher achievement and reduces crime.

The only thing resembling a national strategy to help young children is Head Start, the federal government's primary early education, health services, and nutrition program for low-income children. Unfortunately, because it is chronically underfunded, it can serve only 60 percent of the children eligible for it.[22] Democrats are trying to remedy this situation and increase funding, but the first bill was vetoed by President Bush.

Although Head Start is popular with moderate Republicans and most Democrats in Congress, President Bush has tried to undermine it by folding it into a block grant and turning it over to the states. This could weaken the program by eliminating stringent federal standards, forcing it to compete with other deserving programs and adding huge administrative costs.

I've been trying for decades to do more for our kids, but making progress hasn't been easy. After my second daughter was born, I was lying in the hospital bed wondering how I was going to manage caring for two children while working a very full schedule. I wanted to use my position as a legislator to help other women facing similar struggles. That's when I came up with a package of child-care bills in the New York City Council, called the Virginia

My colleague Representative Lynn Woolsey (D-CA) is a true champion for children and working moms.

She introduced the Family and Workplace Balancing Act. It's a holistic legislative package aimed at comprehensively addressing the work/life balance needs of millions of Americans.

Lynn knows from experience how unexpectedly those needs can arise, particularly for single moms. When she was 29, her husband left her with their three children and little else. She was employed. She and her children went on public assistance for help in paying for food, health insurance, and child care. In one calendar year, she had to resort to 13 different child-care arrangements.

As she wrote in a press statement introducing the act, "[I]t's amazing to me that here we are 35 years later ... the economy and the family have changed radically ... working mothers are the rule rather than the exception ... but public policy still

plan after my new baby. The Virginia plan would have made child care more affordable and available. As a House member, I've introduced initiatives (including legislation that would have allowed *all* child-care expenses to be deducted from a family's taxes as if they were business expenses), held town hall meetings, and discussed child care in hundreds of speeches.

Twenty years later, I'm still trying to build support to expand the availability of high-quality, affordable child care. Last year brought some long-awaited momentum, as the House passed two of my amendments to provide financing for child-care facilities. As of December 2007, they were both awaiting action by the Senate.

I remain hopeful that we will begin to expand support for child care, but services continue to lag behind the need. Fortunately, state and local governments are implementing promising new programs. I find it encouraging that

hasn't caught up. We have little meaningful child-care assistance; we have no paid leave; in fact, we have no respect for the challenges of raising a family today; we have no recognition that there is no more important job than parenting."

The "Balancing Act" addresses everything from the need for universal preschool and after-school programs to pension and health benefits for part-time workers, and a lot more. It would be as expensive as it is extensive. But the investment in our kids and the empowerment of working moms would be worth every penny and more than pay for itself in the long run.

Given the expense, however, it's likely that its components or similar bills in Congress will be passed in a piecemeal fashion, if at all.

It's going to require a lot of persistent grassroots support, and I hope that will include yours.

19

two red states (traditionally conservative), Georgia and Oklahoma, have begun state-funded preschool programs that are open to all four-year-olds.

In Georgia, 80 percent of four-years-olds are enrolled in a state-funded preschool. Among the children attending these preschools, school-readiness scores greatly improved and the skills gap between more- and less-affluent children was eliminated.[23]

Oklahoma's program has enrolled nearly two-thirds of eligible children, and that figure rises to three-fourths if you include kids who are enrolled in Head Start. A university study found that Oklahoma's program improved the school-readiness scores of all children who participated, especially low-income, African American, and Hispanic children.[24]

Of course, guaranteed permanent and wide-ranging work flexibility for families is the ideal, and we are a long way from realizing it. Consider:

- Nationwide, only 52 percent of private-sector employees are entitled to paid sick days.[25]

- At least 37 countries have policies guaranteeing parents some type of paid leave specifically for when their children are ill; the United States does not.[26]

- In a 2002 survey, nearly half of the low-income working parents interviewed had been fired, suspended, denied a promotion, or warned at least once by an employer for taking time off to meet family needs.[27]

- One-quarter of all American adults under age 32 currently are or have been responsible for the long-term care of a family member or friend.[28]

- Three-quarters of Americans say they have no control over their work schedules.[29]

- Nationwide, 54 percent of children under the age of three are in formal child-care centers.[30]

LACTIVATE!

In May 2005, I organized what turned out to be my favorite press conference of all time. It brought together a new breed of activists supporting lactation rights.

I became involved in the "lactivist" movement upon hearing reports of women being ejected from public places just for trying to feed their infants. One park ranger threw a woman out of a national park for breastfeeding because, he told her, it would attract bees. Another woman was ejected from the National Gallery of Art for breastfeeding while looking at a painting of a woman with an exposed breast (you can't make this stuff up). A third was ordered off a New York City subway train.

I also heard numerous stories about difficulties in the workplace, including one of a woman whose male colleagues mooed outside the door as she expressed milk to take home and another of a woman being banished to do so in her car across the street from her office.

At the press conference, "lactivists" conducted a "nurse-in" to support the Breast Feeding Promotion Act, a bill I introduced that would give a tax break to businesses that establish private lactation areas and to mothers who purchase breastfeeding equipment, would protect breastfeeding under civil rights laws, and would create performance standards for breast pumps. As I looked at all of those women and their bundles of joy doing the most natural thing in the world out in the open, I knew that somewhere, Mother Nature was smiling.

I love lactivism because it is so important to infants' health and mothers' peace of mind. Whether or not to breastfeed is a choice that should be freely made by women well informed about the benefits of breastfeeding and not impeded by a regressive employer. In the late 1990s, I successfully worked to gain additional funding for breastfeeding promotion in a federal child nutrition program and to guarantee the right of women to breastfeed

on federal property. Today, the breastfeeding page on my Web site, http://
maloney.house.gov, gets more hits than the page for almost any other issue.

Two conflicting definitions of decency collide over breastfeeding. One
is puritanical; the other is supportive of committed, educated, and compassionate mothers.

The more we defer to the dictates of misguided puritanical attitudes,
which are based on the implicit belief that a woman's body is sexual above all
else, the more breastfeeding will remain in the shadows. And the more it is
instilled with this stigma of shamefulness, the fewer mothers will choose it.

The best way to end the stigma attached to breastfeeding in public is
for the public to get used to it. That will, hopefully, stop colleagues' moo-
ing, help make the workplace work for families, and prevent our infants
from having to eat in a bathroom stall.

Breastfed children:

- Have a lower incidence of sudden infant death syndrome (SIDS)

- Are less likely to suffer from ear infections and respiratory tract infections

- Have fewer digestive problems

- Are less likely to have type 1 (juvenile-onset) diabetes [31]

- May even score higher on intelligence tests[32]

Women who have breastfed:[33]

- Are less likely to develop ovarian and premenopausal breast cancers

- Have less risk of osteoporosis

- Recover more quickly from childbirth

- Are more likely to return to their prepregnancy weight

- Have less risk of long-term obesity

A 1999 study estimated that 3.6 to 7 billion excess dollars are spent every
year on conditions and diseases that are preventable by breastfeeding.[34]

What's good for the bottom line and good for families? Paid parental and sick leave, flexible work schedules, and access to child care. Despite the proven effectiveness of these benefits in increasing worker productivity, retention, and recruitment, the United States has been reluctant to join the rest of the industrialized world in implementing policies to develop these programs. In June 2007, the Government Accountability Office issued a report that I requested entitled "Women and Low-Skilled Workers: Other Countries' Policies and Practices That May Help These Workers Enter and Remain in the Labor Force," showing that other countries have a broader range of workplace benefits, flexibility, and training initiatives and spend more government resources on these programs.[35]

FAMILY-FRIENDLY REPORT CARD: F+

A 2004 Harvard study looked at how the United States ranks among the world's nations in providing programs and policies benefiting children and parents. Here is how we fared.

Paid Leave for Childbearing and Child Rearing[36]

Benefits: Paid leave improves children's health outcomes, facilitates breastfeeding, lowers the infant mortality rate (ours is the highest among the industrialized countries), improves the economic status of families, and enhances both employee productivity and economic returns to employers.

Where we rank: We're tied for last. One hundred sixty-three countries guarantee paid leave to women for childbirth and related events; like Lesotho, Swaziland, and Papua New Guinea, we don't.

Right to Breastfeed or Pump Breast Milk in Private-Sector Workplaces

Benefits: Babies who are breastfed for more than 16 weeks are five times less likely to die of SIDS than babies breastfed for less than 4 weeks.[37] There is also evidence that it lowers the risk of later developing obesity, leukemia, breast cancer, and asthma and boosts IQ.

Where we rank: We're tied for last. The United States isn't among the 107 countries that protect this right.

Early Childhood Education and Care

Benefits: Having high-quality education and care in early childhood improves academic performance and therefore economic potential over

Sometimes, I'm tempted to send a thank-you note to someone who commits an RAOC—a Revealing Act of Candor—that exposes gender bias in the workplace. But in 2005, advertising giant WPP director Neil French killed so many birds with one stone in illustrating how working mothers are discriminated against that I almost sent him a bouquet of flowers.

When asked before a crowd of 300 advertising executives why women creative directors are notoriously rare, he reportedly argued that it was because they were not good enough. He went on to describe female creative directors as "crap" who would inevitably "wimp out and go suckle something."

In follow-up interviews, French defended his statements. "[T]o be a creative director requires 100 percent commitment," he said. "People who have babies to look after can't do that." Women, he said, "don't work hard enough. It's not a joke job. The future

the life span, and it reduces the need for special education programs, repeating grades, and run-ins with the criminal justice system.

Where we rank: We're tied with Suriname and Ecuador for 39th— behind every Western European county except Finland.

Guaranteed Leave for Parents to Attend Teacher Conferences

Benefits: Parental involvement in a child's education results in higher test scores, better behavior in school, more studying, and a lower likelihood of dropping out.

Where we rank: We're tied for last. At least 34 countries guarantee this right, 17 of them with pay.

of the entire agency is in your hands as creative director."

French's comments gathered together every misconception and prejudice that leads to the wage gap: that working mothers are incapable of giving 100 percent to their jobs, that women take "joke" jobs so they can balance work and family (leading to their marginalization in the workforce), that you can't have any outside responsibilities if you want to be a senior executive, that women are intrinsically less talented than men, that breastfeeding is worthy of mockery, and that motherhood itself is trivial.

After French resigned from WPP, I learned something that floored me: Despite the fact that women make 83 percent of all purchases in America, they make up only 3 percent of all senior executives at advertising firms.[38]

You call this progress?

Take-Action Guide

A Workplace That Works for Families

Creating a family-friendly workplace is everyone's responsibility. Employers, employees, the government, and *you* must all get involved. Stay abreast of legislation that affects these issues and urge your representatives to support them, get involved in initiatives at your own workplace, and work at the grassroots level to address these issues in your own backyard. Here are some ways to get started.

1. Work to end wage discrimination.

• **Join or start a WAGE Club.** The WAGE Project is a nonprofit group working to end workplace discrimination against women. To join WAGE in this effort, simply get together a group of interested women, download a WAGE Club Discussion Guide, and start. Go to www. wageproject.org.

• **Know what you need to know, do what you need to do.** The American Association of University Women has an excellent pay equity resource kit that will help you understand the wage gap and empower you to do something about it. It's available at www.aauw.org/advocacy/issue_advocacy/actionpages/upload/ payequityResourceKit.pdf.

• **Encourage your senior management to conduct a gender equity audit.** Business and Professional Women/USA used a US Department of Labor document to devise a questionnaire that helps employers gauge their performance. Download it from www.bpwusa.org/files/ public/EqualPayAudit2006.doc.

• **Demand what you're worth.** Salary.com will help you determine the average, high, and low ranges for a given job by location, experience, and education. Then, use one of the many guides available online to learn to negotiate a higher rate; www.wageproject.org, and www. careerjournal.com/salaryhiring/negotiate/20040330-patterson.html are good places to start.

• **Discuss, educate, network.** There are many wonderful e-mail lists and blogs out there that deal with work issues related to women. Try Women's Lunch Talk (http://womensmedia.com/lunchtalk) and the Women at Work Network blog (http://womenatworknetwork. blogspot.com).

• **Urge your congresspeople to pass the Paycheck Fairness Act.** See the National Committee on Pay Equity's Web site at www.pay-equity. org/info-leg.html for details on this act. The WAGE Project's site also has an advocacy section on current laws, pending court cases, proposed legislation, and news coverage: www.wageproject.org/ content/reality/advocate.php.

2. Help create workplaces that work for families so parents have the flexibility they need to balance work and care.

• **Gain flexibility for yourself.** Work Options (www.workoptions. com) offers customizable proposal templates for requesting a change from a full-time schedule to a compressed workweek, part-time flexible schedule, telecommuter position, and shared-job arrangement. The University of California Hastings College of the Law WorkLife Law Center's Web site provides valuable legal information on employees' rights as caregivers: www.worklifelaw. org. If your company does not have a policy accommodating caregivers, give your human resources representative the

National Organization for Women's "employer pledge" for a
woman-friendly workplace as a starting point: www.now.org/
issues/wfw/empledge.html.

• **Advocate for a more woman-friendly workplace.** Host a house
party to screen *The Motherhood Manifesto*, a documentary
produced by MomsRising, to educate, entertain, and inspire
friends, co-workers, and neighbors to work toward family-friendly
policies and legislation: www.momsrising.org/party. Mothers and
More (www.mothersandmore.org) is an organization of more than
7,500 members in 150 chapters across the country. Members
participate in everything from organized socializing to issues-
based advocacy on the challenges of balancing family
and work.

• **Work with groups in your state to support or initiate family-
friendly legislation, such as California's Paid Family Leave
Program.** Learn about both national- and state-level legislative issues
affecting family and medical leave from the National Partnership for
Women and Families (www.nationalpartnership.org). MomsRising
(www.momsrising.org) tracks legislation related to maternity and
paternity leave, flexible work, health care, child care, wages, and even
entertainment standards. If you belong to a labor union, the Labor
Project for Working Families (www.laborproject.org) works with
unions and other organizations to secure family-friendly work
policies.

• **Urge your federal legislators to support the Family and
Workplace Balancing Act** sponsored by Representative Lynn
Woolsey. The National Organization for Women has
a summary of the bill on their Web site (www.now.org/lists/

now-action-list/msg00239.html), and you can also sign up for e-mail alerts on issues affecting women.

• **Support my two Family and Medical Leave Act expansion bills and the Working Families Flexibility Act.** The Family and Medical Leave Inclusion Act would amend the FMLA to guarantee unpaid leave to care for a domestic partner, parent-in-law, adult child, sibling, or grandparent who has a serious health condition. The Family and Medical Leave Enhancement Act would broaden FMLA protections from employees of companies with 50 or more workers to those of companies with more than 25. It would also allow employees who are parents or grandparents to meet their family's education and health-care needs by taking up to 24 hours of leave during any 12-month period to go to parent-teacher conferences or to take family members to regular medical or dental appointments. The Working Families Flexibility Act protects a worker's right to ask for a work schedule modification without fear of retribution. Visit my Web site, http://maloney.house.gov, to learn more.

3. Help give every mother in the workplace the rights and resources she needs to encourage her to breastfeed.

• **Support my Breastfeeding Promotion Act.** This act would amend the Civil Rights Act of 1964 to protect breastfeeding by new mothers, provide tax incentives for businesses to provide a private breastfeeding area, develop a performance standard for breast pumps, and allow a tax deduction for breastfeeding equipment. Go to my Web site (http://maloney.house.gov) for more information.

• **Support lactation.** The La Leche League (www.llli.org) provides exceptional informational support for mothers who are breastfeeding.

It also tracks state and federal laws related to breastfeeding and gathers in one place information about issues, policies, and advocacy opportunities, at www.lllusa.org/advocacy.php. Promotion of Mother's Milk (ProMoM) offers at www.promom.org/bf_info/bf_work.html a sample letter that mothers who need better breastfeeding accommodations at work can give to their human resources representatives.

2

★ ★ ★

THE IMBALANCE
OF POWER

"Our struggle today is not to have a female Einstein get appointed as an assistant professor. It is for a woman schlemiel to get as quickly promoted as a male schlemiel."

—BELLA ABZUG

SEXUAL HARASSMENT =
OCCUPATIONAL SEGREGATION

Until I was elected to public office and became the boss myself, sexual harassment for me was just part of the job. A man who was interviewing me for a position in the 1970s asked me to remove my blouse and skirt and stand sideways for him so he could "look at [my] figure." I passed on the request and the job.

Many people, especially men, don't realize that sexual harassment isn't just a nuisance. It creates a hostile work environment that drives women out of jobs, particularly blue-collar ones, and it's one of the main factors behind occupational segregation. According to the Women's Bureau of the US Department of Labor, "Tradeswomen often cite sexual harassment and

One day, I got an e-mail from Elyse, who works at a global shipping company based in the Pacific Northwest that frequently shows up on "best places for women to work" lists.

She conducts orientation for new employees and makes it a point to monitor how women are treated on the shipping floor. She told me that even at her company, only about 1 of every 10 women lasts on the floor. Sexual harassment is one reason why.

Women who are being sexually harassed often go to Elyse for advice and advocacy. "I choose to pick the battles of my employees who are being grabbed, intimidated, and insulted," she explained. "If I reported every stupid, sexist comment that I heard, the company would eventually think I'm a reactionary. ... Sometimes it seems easier to just look at them and shake my head."

Elyse believes that the vast majority of harassment goes unreported, in part because it can come back to haunt the accuser. When she reported a male colleague for making lewd tongue gestures, her bosses confronted her. They told her they were trying to develop a "team atmosphere" and suggested that she was undermining it.

She says even repeat offenders aren't fired. They're just rotated to another area.

That's how it works at a company that has a "strict zero-tolerance policy."

discrimination as reasons for why they leave the trades, and young women cite fear of sexual harassment as a reason for not choosing trades as a career."

US Supreme Court nominee Clarence Thomas's confirmation hearings before the Senate Judiciary Committee in 1991 were a watershed moment for awareness about sexual harassment in the workplace. After University of Oklahoma law professor Anita Hill testified that Thomas had sexually harassed her after she refused to date him, a huge number of women came up to me on the street and said things like "They're finally talking about it!" Then they launched into tales of their own sordid experiences.

Sexual harassment complaints skyrocketed following the Thomas hearings. But rumors of the demeaning behavior's defeat have been greatly exaggerated.

Blue-collar women in particular are often held to unfair attendance and performance standards, excluded from the training they need, and denied the kind of assistance that men routinely receive from their male co-workers.

That's exactly what happened to firefighter Adrienne Walsh when she joined the elite Rescue Company 4 of Queens, New York. A Coast Guard reservist, champion distance runner, and veteran of the September 11 attacks on the World Trade Center, Adrienne earned her posting to the elite company with outstanding performance. But New York's *Daily News* reported that instead of a welcoming reception, she was met with harassment and ostracism. She got threatening phone calls. Her co-workers refused to speak to her, even about job-related matters. Rumors swirled about her abilities. She requested a transfer back to a regular company after just five weeks.

Patricia Fitzpatrick told me about Adrienne during a tribute to firefighters who had given their lives on 9/11 that was held at a firehouse in my district. Patricia had been one of the 45 women in the first co-ed class of firefighters hired in 1982. She told me that only 51 women firefighters had been hired since then; today, there are 317 male firefighters for every woman.[1]

She believes it's a self-perpetuating cycle. Women don't join the fire department because they have seen what happened to those who went before. "Whenever there is press about a woman in the fire service, it has to do with her being harassed," she said.

As Joan Williams, professor of law and director of the Center for Work Life Law at the University of California Hastings College of the Law in San Francisco, has pointed out, notions of a "man's job" and "woman's work" have provided a psychological refuge for blue-collar men who have seen their wages fall in terms of real value since the 1970s. Most can no longer support their families on their incomes alone.[2] Women's attempts to break into "men's jobs" have only added what some men perceive as insult to injury. This resentment, however understandable, has had terrible consequences, from sexual harassment to grudging tokenism to the dismal representation of women in blue-collar professions.

Fortunately, tough women out there are successfully swimming upstream. Caro Marrero, an East Harlem carpenter who lives in my former City Council district, contacted me about the gender-related challenges she faces.

She goes the extra mile to overcome intense scrutiny and skepticism about the ability of a woman to do her job. "If you're a male mechanic and the foreman likes you, you can stay working for years," she told me. "It doesn't mean you're a great mechanic. Unfortunately for women, it doesn't work that way."

Caro has fended off the sexual harassment she encounters. A male worker once asked her to wear perfume on the job because he "didn't like smelling stinky men."

"I told him, 'They sell something called scented candles,'" Caro recounted. "'Why don't you go to the store and light them in your work area?' He just looked at me, and then his friend

- Women filed 10,174 sexual harassment complaints with the Equal Employment Opportunity Commission (EEOC) in 2006, compared with 9,574 in 1992.[3]

- In 2003, fewer than 2 percent of boilermakers, bricklayers, carpenters, ironworkers, machinists, masons, mechanics, operating engineers, painters, and sheet metal workers were women.[4]

STANDING UP WHILE THE EEOC STANDS DOWN

In the late 1990s, I held an unofficial "field" hearing in New York City to investigate sex discrimination on Wall Street.

said, 'That's a nice way of saying, "@#&! you,"' and I said, 'Basically, yes.'"

Caro's career is also threatened by her need to balance work and family. "It's a man's world," she told me. "We don't have paid sick days. If your kid is sick, you can take a week off if you want. It doesn't mean that when you want to come back, they will take you back."

Four times in one year, Caro had to change babysitters. She told me that the lack of affordable child care is driving women from the workforce. "When you have to pay $150 a week for day care, sometimes working just isn't worth it. If I didn't have the support I have, I wouldn't be able to [work]. I love my job, but if it came between my family and my job, I'd have to go with my family."

That's a decision no woman should have to make.

There, I met Allison Schieffelin, a highly successful bond salesperson at Morgan Stanley, one of the biggest investment banks.

At the time, Allie had just filed a complaint with the EEOC for being passed over for promotion because of her gender. Allie alleged that after a dinner with important clients, she was sent home so that her male colleagues could take the clients to a strip club. It was a perfect reflection of the pervasive old boys' network on Wall Street. After making the allegation, she was fired, despite having logged almost 15 successful years at the firm.

As she put it, "Morgan Stanley destroyed my career. They destroyed everything that I had put my heart and soul into for 15 years." Allie says she sacrificed her personal life (her marriage ended in divorce) to put in long hours and go the extra mile for the firm, which is often required of women for them to be regarded as equals.

Most worrisome, Allie's case wasn't an isolated incident. Her EEOC complaint mushroomed into a class action sex discrimination case against the firm. More than 20 women were prepared to testify that they had been the victims of salacious behavior and sexual harassment. Morgan Stanley settled the case before the women took the stand, agreeing to pay $54 million in damages: $12 million to Allie, $40 million earmarked for 300 other mid- and high-level female employees (though only 67 filed claims), and $2 million to fund workplace diversity and antidiscrimination programs.[5]

You might think that Morgan Stanley would work especially hard to eradicate sex discrimination after so costly an episode. But the firm settled another class action sex discrimination suit in 2007 for $46 million[6]—bringing its overall sex discrimination price tag to an even $100 million. That sounds like a lot, but it only amounts to a few good days of trading.

Despite these incidents, Morgan Stanley has been cited numerous times by *Working Mother* magazine as one of the 100 Best Companies for Working Mothers. That makes me wonder how bad things are at other companies.

Wall Street is hardly alone. Discrimination against women permeates numerous industries. We're practically surrounded by it. If you drive your Mitsubishi to the airport after filling its tank at Sunoco, board a Boeing-built plane for a United Airlines flight, use your Verizon cell phone service to call your spouse before you take off, and then bite into a Krispy Kreme doughnut, you've just enriched six household-name companies that have settled or lost sex discrimination cases and lawsuits in recent years.

I greatly admire the women who step forward to sue for harassment, but I don't envy them. As Jocelyn Larkin, the attorney representing 1.5 million women Wal-Mart employees in the largest sex discrimination suit in history, told me, "Unless your upside is an enormous amount of money, why would you [file suit] if it's the case that 'you won't work in this town again'?"

The Bush administration has made it harder to bring such a case, reducing the EEOC to what its union called a "shell of an agency."[7] Between 2001 and 2007, the EEOC lost 25 percent of its staff due to a hiring freeze.[8] Even worse, under a pilot program, a privatized national call center manned by minimally trained telemarketers replaced experienced EEOC investigators in answering employee complaints. Despite the fact that the Office of the Inspector General deemed the call center ineffective, EEOC commissioners voted to extend the pilot program. Not surprisingly, the slash-and-burn outsourcing of civil rights enforcement has led to higher backlogs, longer delays, and a steep drop in the percentage of cases in which the EEOC has found "cause" for complainants to pursue a discrimination case.[9]

For the past several years, many EEOC employees have worn black on the day after the fiscal year ends to mark it as a "day of mourning." It includes a moment of silence for "lost charges"—cases that were closed just prior to the year's end without having been investigated.

Fortunately, refusing to stand by and let civil rights rest in peace, Senator Barbara Mikulski (D-MD) inserted a $50 million windfall increase in the EEOC's budget into an appropriations bill through a sub-committee she chairs[10]—demonstrating once again that a woman's place is in the House and the Senate. As this book went to press, the bill had passed in the Senate.

MIND THE GAP

At Wal-Mart and many other companies, asking how much other people are paid is grounds for termination.

Meditate on that for a minute. Under the law, employers are obligated to provide equal pay for equal work, but they are allowed to fire anyone who tries to discover whether they are actually receiving equal pay for equal work.

The Paycheck Fairness Act—federal legislation sponsored by Senator Hillary Rodham Clinton (D-NY) and Representative Rosa DeLauro (D-CT)—would end this workplace gag rule.

In addition to supporting federal measures to ensure pay equity, you can also urge the senior management at your own workplace to conduct a gender equity audit. This type of survey looks at factors such as compensation, what proportion of senior executive and board positions are held by women, layoff trends, whether expenses incurred at establishments that exclude or exploit women are reimbursed

Equal-pay activist and former lieutenant governor of Massachusetts Evelyn Murphy spent eight years documenting hundreds of sex discrimination cases in every corner of American society—not just business, but government and academia, too. In conjunction with publishing her authoritative book on the wage gap, Getting Even: Why Women Don't Get Paid Like Men and What to Do About It, *she launched the WAGE (Women Are Getting Even) Project.*

From coast to coast, the initiative has spawned WAGE Clubs, groups of women who get together to identify whether they are being paid fairly at work and strategize about what to do if they are not. The WAGE Project offers the best resources I've come across to help women fight the wage gap.

When I spoke to Evelyn in 2005, she offered this top-line advice. "What women have to do to go in to their employers [to demand equal pay] is do the research, benchmark their salaries, learn what people are being paid [at that same level] in the company. Interestingly enough, [at many companies] there's a lot of talk that goes on. Without doing anything inappropriate or illegal, most guys know what other guys are making. Women just don't talk about it very much. But if you start talking and find your allies, a group of allies, that all feel that some women are being paid unfairly, assemble a group of people to go talk to the top boss. Just go right to the top. If you go to the HR people or the middle managers, you're never going to get anywhere."

(most Wall Street firms no longer reimburse for excursions to strip clubs), and the prevalence of sexual discrimination and harassment complaints.

Internal audits like these are helpful, but requiring public disclosure would be ideal. The Massachusetts Institute of Technology, the State of Minnesota, and Ben & Jerry's disclose the results of their periodic gender equity audits, but I don't know of a single publicly held company that does. As Martha Burk, former executive director of the National Council of Women's Organizations (NCWO), says in her book *Cult of Power*, "Making gender equity audits public ought to be viewed as a basic fairness tool. While companies can learn virtually everything about employees, from traffic tickets to health conditions, employees can learn almost nothing about employer behavior that affects them fundamentally."

VALUING LIVES

As I watched black smoke billowing from the Pentagon on September 11, all I could think about was the only place I wanted to be: home. By the time House majority leader Dick Armey (R-TX) ordered all personnel to evacuate the Capitol, I was already in a rental car heading north. I tried to reach my husband and daughters, but the phone lines were jammed. Electronic signs on the New Jersey Turnpike read "Turn Back" and "No Entry to New York" and "Emergency Vehicles Only." Traffic thinned until it was almost all emergency vehicles traveling toward the city.

The gap in New York's spectacular skyline where the towers had stood came into view. Watching the black smoke pour out of the void and blow eastward over Wall Street, I knew I was returning to a city that would never be the same.

I was greatly relieved, although not surprised, to find my husband and daughters safe and sound. After holding them long and tight, I got the strangest urge, probably born of a yearning for normalcy on a day that had thrust New York into uncharted territory—to see if the subway was running. Lo and behold, despite the fact that one of its stops no longer existed and other stations had been heavily damaged, the trains were rolling into East 86th Street as they would on any other day. To me, it was the first heartening sign that New York was going to find a way to get through this.

My district lost approximately 500 souls. With each day that passed, I learned more about who they were. One was a college friend of my daughter's—one of the smartest, sunniest, and most optimistic people I've ever met—who was thriving at her first job. Almost all of the firefighters from a firehouse on Roosevelt Island, which is in my district, went into the towers and never came out.

Amid all the grief, trauma, and upheaval, amid all the desperate needs that had to be met, I was stupefied when victims' families were confronted with one issue that I never would have dreamed would arise in connection with 9/11: the wage gap.

After the attacks, Congress quickly passed legislation creating the Victim Compensation Fund to provide financial assistance to victims' families. The amount of compensation would be calculated based on the estimated lifetime earnings of a deceased worker. The more the deceased had earned, the greater the amount that would go to the victim's family.

The problem was that the "Special Master" in charge of the Victim Compensation Fund, attorney Kenneth Feinberg, was calculating estimated lifetime earnings using outdated gender-based insurance tables. The tables reflected the historical wage gap. For example, if a man and a woman had the same work history, the same job, and the same annual salary of $35,000, the woman's family would receive $175,000 less than the man's.

The wage gap was such a basic part of life that the federal government viewed it not as an injustice but as a given.

With help from the National Organization for Women, I organized 11 members of the New York congressional delegation to compose and sign a letter demanding that the US Department of Justice eliminate this outrageous discrimination.

Ultimately, we were successful, and the injustice was corrected.

But insurance companies across the country are still using these tables to calculate benefits in wrongful death and injury cases.

You call this progress?

• Economist Evan Schouten estimates that in wrongful death lawsuits, the lifetime economic value of a 30-year-old homemaker is only about $300,000—more than $1 million less than the value of an average white-collar worker.[11]

WOMEN NEED NOT APPLY . . . STILL!

If you enjoy raining on a crowd-pleasing parade, coming face to face with the Ku Klux Klan, and being the least popular person in town, then you should have been in Augusta, Georgia, with me in April 2002. The NCWO was hosting a rally during the storied Masters Golf Tournament.

Two busloads of women's rights advocates descended on the Augusta National Golf Club. We were there to protest the ultimate symbol of exclu-

After working as a cashier for a year and garnering excellent performance reviews, Wal-Mart employee Betty Dukes was given a pay raise, then promoted to a "managerial" (though not salaried) position a few years later.

That, she claims, was when her head hit glass. A major cause of the sudden halt in her advancement was what she called a "tap on the shoulder" approach to promotions. Absent formal criteria for selection, store managers had the freedom to promote based largely on discretion. A hiring pattern evolved that resulted in overwhelming gender disparities. Male managers were more likely to promote from within their informal network, which was disproportionately male.

Betty also was denied management training that was routinely offered to younger, less experienced male employees. She protested to no avail. She was eventually demoted back to cashier.

She filed a lawsuit against Wal-Mart. This initial shot across Wal-Mart's bow evolved into the largest class action sex discrimination suit in American history, with 1.5 million plaintiffs.

Thanks to Betty and others like her, Wal-Mart's lawyers will have to explain why 65 percent of the company's hourly workers, but only 33 percent of its managers, are women. They'll also be asked why job reviews across the company showed that women who weren't being promoted consistently outperformed men who were.[12]

In February 2007, the US 9th Circuit Court of Appeals affirmed a lower court's 2004 decision to let the case move forward as a class action lawsuit. Wal-Mart is appealing the decision.

Who says one woman can't make a difference?

sion: the men-only social club. Augusta National's membership includes hundreds of the most powerful men in corporate America—but women need not apply.

The rally was just one event in a much larger effort to expose the exclusivity that continues to hold women back.

Although most people associate Augusta National with the Masters, it's not just a golf course. It's also where billions of dollars of business transactions are conceived and discussed and where invitations to join boards, companies, and powerful business associations are extended.

Months before the rally, former NCWO executive director Martha Burk tried to persuade Augusta to open the club to women by sending a letter to Augusta National's then-chairman, William "Hootie" Johnson.

"We know that Augusta National and the sponsors of the Masters do not want to be viewed as entities that tolerate discrimination against any group, including women," she wrote. "We urge you to review your policies and practices in this regard, and open your membership to women now, so that this is not an issue when the tournament is staged next year."

Johnson dashed off a letter in response. "I have found your letter's several references to discrimination, allusions to the sponsors and your setting of deadlines to be both offensive and coercive. I hope you will understand why any further communication between us would not be productive."

So Martha embarked on a strategy that would be "productive." She created an alliance of women's groups, members of Congress, editorial boards, and the female employees of companies whose top executives held Augusta National memberships.

At several companies, including Citigroup and American Express, employees met with their CEOs to complain. While some of the men professed support for female membership in principle and gave assurances that they would work for change within the club, only one corporate official, former CBS executive Thomas H. Wyman, resigned his membership.[13] (In addition, John Snow, who was the nominee for secretary of the US Treasury at the time, resigned from Augusta one hour after United Press International's Helen Thomas, the first lady of the White House press corps, raised the issue at a White House press briefing.)

I know plenty of Fortune 500 CEOs. Most of them are fine people. But they obviously didn't feel as strongly about the issue as I'd hoped they would. Considering the scarcity of women in boardrooms and corner offices, I should have known better than to overestimate their commitment.

Going into the Augusta battle, I had a grand vision of a photo op featuring a co-ed foursome of CEOs teeing off at Augusta's hallowed first hole. I really thought it was going to happen. That vision of women amid the azaleas, awash in lush green grass, morphed into the reality of brown mud caked on my heels at the end of the rally.

We had fought hard and well, but to no avail. All that was left to do was to return to Washington and take up the battle there.

At my request, the Joint Committee on Taxation compiled estimates that showed that business tax deductions for money spent on gender-exclusive (same-sex) clubs cost American taxpayers about $5 million a year. I introduced a bill that would have forbidden companies from deducting expenses incurred at same-sex clubs.

Some women have asked me why I've devoted time and effort to a country club that has only several hundred members. Let the boys go have their fun, they say.

Your tax dollars aren't just covering martinis in Augusta's grill room. In 2003, Robert McCormick, CEO of information technology infrastructure services company Savvis, allegedly put $241,000 on his American Express corporate card at Scores, a strip club in my district. Under federal law, half of those "business" expenses were tax deductible. After American Express sued for nonpayment in 2005, Savvis asked a New York court to dismiss the suit because the services were not legitimate business expenses. The company's board of directors accepted McCormick's resignation and negotiated a settlement with American Express.

Rather than being asked to underwrite lap dances at strip clubs through tax deductions, I believe taxpayers would prefer to see their tax dollars cover real business expenses that families incur when they pay for child care, which allows them to work outside the home. That's why I've introduced legislation to make most child-care expenses tax deductible.

I do it because Augusta is the tip of a very damaging iceberg. Old boys' networks aren't confined to senior executives and fancy country clubs. They span all echelons of the workforce.

It is everyone's job to identify them. If you're a member of a gender-exclusive club, it's time to resign. If you've been excluded from one, it's time to break in.

That's how opportunity expands.

• One survey found that lack of access to male networks, persistent stereotypes, and a shortage of mentors and role models for women are the three main reasons that corporate America remains predominately male at the very top.[14]

THE ♂ NETWORK

But as important as it is for women to break into men's networks, we must also do more to create our own. As Goldman Sachs partner Josephine Linden told me, "One of the things that women don't do very well is network and bring in a circle of people they know to try and help them improve and develop and be promoted. That's where I think men do a really good job."

It's strange: Women are an underrepresented minority in the upper reaches of the workplace, and most underrepresented minorities recognize the need to band together to increase their representation. Yet "male bonding" is common, and women haven't traditionally used our strong friendship circles to succeed in business. In the workplace, this costs women dearly.

Some leading-edge companies, including Goldman Sachs, have instituted formal women's networks. Industry associations can also serve as powerful networks. The Financial Women's Association (FWA) of New York underscores the progress women *have* made in the workplace, especially when they support one another. The organization boasts close to 1,000 members, of whom more than 40 percent earn more than $200,000 per year. Eight out of 10 hold C-suite and other officer-level positions in their companies, and more than 50 percent have net worths that exceed $1 million.

My neighbor Susan Lyne, CEO of Martha Stewart Living, demonstrates the kind of solidarity with women that we need to see more of. She sent to headhunters a list of 100 women who would make great board members. She told me that in the wake of corporate governance scandals like those involving Enron and WorldCom, "there's not a board out there that is not looking for women to bring on. For a long time, board members just recommended their friends. It was a fairly closed world. But now they have headhunters who are doing a much better job of identifying female candidates."

You might not know 1 person, let alone 100, who is qualified to serve on a corporate board. But if we all apply the spirit of Susan's advice at the organization and level we work at, we can effect dramatic changes for women at every level of the workforce, in both white-collar and blue-collar settings.

Be magnanimous in telling managers about women colleagues who are doing a great job and ought to be considered for the next promotion (or spared in the next downsizing). Encourage talented women to take the next step. This is networking in action, and it pays back in spades.

Still, it is well established that one component of the wage gap is that women don't negotiate as often or as hard as men do. Tory Johnson, CEO of Women for Hire, which provides an array of recruitment services for women, puts it well: "Men see negotiations as a game; women liken it to root canal," she says. "Therefore, they take what is offered, preferring not to rock the boat."

Fortunately, networking and learning or teaching how to negotiate are two things that you can do today to get more immediate results in closing the wage gap for yourself and womankind (see the box on the opposite page).

Take-Action Guide

The Imbalance of Power

We need to tackle discrimination in a way that defeats occupational seg-regation, gets women's careers off the basement floor, and shatters the glass ceiling. Together, we can close the wage gap, increase opportunities for women, and grow our economy for everyone.

1. Work to give women full and free access to any career they want.

• **Support organizations that fight occupational segregation.** Wider Opportunities for Women (www.wowonline.org) provides information, support, and suggestions for women in nontraditional occupations, especially blue-collar jobs. Women Employed (www. womenemployed.org) helps struggling employed and unemployed women expand beyond traditional "pink ghetto" jobs (such as cashiers, bank tellers, or waitresses). Its principal online tool, Career Coach, helps women identify a good career, plan for getting it, and obtain the training and education necessary to succeed. An advocacy organization called 9to5, National Association of Working Women (www.9to5.org) focuses on federal issues that affect working women's lives, from fighting downsizing at the EEOC to threats to the Family and Medical Leave Act; its Job Survival Hotline helps women seeking fair treatment at work: 800-522-0925 or hotline@9to5.org.

• **Support restoration of EEOC funding to battle discrimination and sexual harassment.** Write to the EEOC's chair, Naomi Earp, and tell her you want EEOC field employees answering complaints, not poorly trained call center employees. (Don't even try calling. If you do, you'll find yourself wading through an aggravating touch-tone bureaucracy—which is exactly why EEOC field officers should be answering the phone!) For alternate contact information, see www.eeoc.gov/contact.html.

Naomi Earp, Chair

US Equal Employment Opportunity Commission

1801 L Street NW

Washington, DC 20507

Also write to your federal legislators and urge them to support Senator Barbara Mikulski's efforts to inject $50 million into the budget to restore the EEOC to its former glory.

2. Shatter the glass ceiling.

• **Get women the mentoring they need to move up.** Build a "personal board of directors" composed of women and men at senior and junior levels of your company. Join a mentoring program in your company— as a mentor *and* a mentee. If no formal program exists, make yourself available to junior colleagues to discuss career strategies and ask your senior colleagues to set aside time for *you*. Look outside your current company for additional mentors. The National Council of Women's Organizations (www.womensorganizations.org) offers New Faces, More Voices, an internship program that fosters mentorship among professional women across companies and organizations.

• **Work to increase women's access to male networks and encourage women to form powerful ones of their own.** Join or start a women's network at your company. Connect with peers and colleagues to collaborate and socialize. Set up group lunches, after-work cocktail hours, and other opportunities for women colleagues to get to know each other as well as women from other organizations in your industry. If you're not always running out of business cards, you're probably not networking enough. Join national networks like the National Association for Female Executives (http://nafe.com), which has chapters in almost every state. Business and Professional Women/ USA provides leadership development classes, educational scholarships for career advancement, and resources for small-business owners and entrepreneurs. Its local chapters afford many opportunities for formal and informal mentoring; find yours at www.bpwusa.org/custom/ state_locals. Women's Prerogative's Web site (www.womensprerogative. org) has an option that instantly connects you with resources for mentoring, socializing, networking, and organizing.

• **Support my Ending Tax Breaks for Discrimination bill** to eliminate tax deductions for business expenses associated with gender-exclusive organizations (like Augusta National Golf Club). Go to my Web site, http://maloney.house.gov, for more on the bill. You can also find out more about the fight to admit women to Augusta at the National Council on Women's Organizations site, www.womensorganizations. org. Support my bill that would make all child-care expenses deductible instead.

• **Feed the pipeline.** Do as Susan Lyne did: Offer talented women's names to headhunters for board seats—www.catalystwomen.org can help at that level. Or, just suggest women colleagues for promotions within your own workplace.

3

EQUAL OPPORTUNITY
FOR ALL

"Laws will not eliminate prejudice from the hearts of human beings. But that is no reason to allow prejudice to continue to be enshrined in our laws—to perpetuate injustice through inaction."

—SHIRLEY CHISHOLM

Research and common sense tell us how important role models are. As we grow, we do better if we have others to emulate.

Since my childhood in North Carolina and Virginia, I've been blessed to have many role models myself. I might never have run for office if I hadn't seen Bella Abzug and Elizabeth Holtzman win seats representing New York in Congress. And it's an honor to serve part of the district in Queens once served by another of my role models, Representative Geraldine Ferraro.

I didn't have the honor of serving in the House with these remarkable women. But other women members of Congress have been wonderful colleagues and amazing sources of guidance and inspiration.

Every member of Congress needs someone to show her the ropes. The House of Representatives is a complex institution with all sorts of traditions, intricacies, and quirks. When I first got there in 1993, I kept finding a bucket of ice outside my office in the morning. Ice buckets were outside other members' offices, too.

It seemed strange, so I asked around and learned something even stranger. Members had received ice buckets every day since before refrigeration, when ice was useful for storing food. Ice delivery created jobs that Congress never got around to cutting, so the deliveries continued long after members had refrigerators in their offices—that shows you how long it can take for things to change in Washington. The ice buckets were finally nixed in 1995.

House floor debates have all sorts of parliamentary rules that can baffle a freshman member as much as the ice buckets initially baffled me. You're surrounded by members who have a full command of those rules and know exactly how to capitalize on them. So, as a freshman, I welcomed any friends or mentors who could give me guidance on how the place worked.

In 1993, right after I had spoken before the House about the Family and Medical Leave Act, I met a woman who was about to become a friend and a mentor. She approached me on the House floor after hearing me talk about my two daughters, and she began asking me questions about them. I told her frankly that I was finding it hard to be the kind of wife and mother I wanted to be, given the long hours and my need to be away from them in Washington so much of the time. She replied that she could relate, to say the least. She had five children, and her district was in California.

Most conversations on the floor are about issues, strategy, and inside scoops. This time, we were just a couple of anonymous working moms far from home, talking about what working moms love to talk about. It was comforting, and it made me feel a little more at home in the House.

I was impressed by my companion's intelligence, wit, vivacity, and heart. But I never could have guessed that she would emerge from the House's sea of suits and ties to sit in the Speaker's chair.

With shrewd, tireless, and disciplined leadership, Nancy Pelosi climbed the legislative ladder during Democrats' darkest days and helped pull our party back from the abyss.

Her path to the Speaker's chair was lined with brambles. She was so maligned during the 2006 campaign that mention of "Speaker Pelosi" became a scare tactic used by conservatives. Fox News commentator Bill O'Reilly warned that if Nancy were elected, her "San Francisco values" (her district includes that city) would wreak havoc on the moral fiber of the nation. But she was tough as nails, and it all bounced right off her.

On January 4, 2007, the day Nancy accepted the Speaker's gavel, she walked around the Capitol flexing the biceps muscle of her right arm, striking the pose of Rosie the Riveter, the woman on the famous World War II–era posters designed to attract women to blue-collar jobs. Nancy even passed out buttons that had her face pasted onto Rosie's body.

But that was inside the Beltway. While I had little doubt that Nancy would knock her swearing-in speech out of the park, I couldn't have predicted the degree to which it would emphasize gender.

When she was finally handed the gavel, Nancy hit a grand slam—for Democrats, for the country, and for women. She was poised, strong, uplifting, exuberant, and, best of all, authentic. She celebrated her achievement as a woman. "For our daughters and granddaughters, today we have broken the marble ceiling," she said. "For our daughters and granddaughters, the sky is the limit, anything is possible for them."

Speaker Pelosi also played up her role as a mother and grandmother. Reportedly, she had asked a House parliamentarian before she gave her speech if kids could be called up to the podium. She was told that calling up anyone other than her own under-age-12 grandkids would be "out of order."

But she did it anyway. She invited all the children in the chamber to come up and touch the gavel. It was quite clear to me that this wasn't a political stunt—although it would have been a good one—but rather a maternal gesture from the heart.

"This is what I've been waiting for," I thought. A woman who breaks the marble ceiling and also breaks the rules."

Now *this* was progress!

THE DAY OF NANCY'S swearing-in was all the more special for me because I got to spend part of it with my greatest mentor from my early days in Congress, Representative Pat Schroeder (D-CO).

Pat served in Congress for 24 years, beginning in 1973. When she got there, there were just 16 women in Congress. Most of her tenure was during what I consider the era of the first generation of women in Congress. Back then, women were more of an oddity than just a minority. That era ended with the "Year of the Woman," as 1992, the year I was elected, was called. That year, the number of women representatives went from 28 to 47, and the number of women senators went from 4 to 7.

Pat fought a lot of lonely battles on women's behalf and also put up with a lot of sexism. After winning a contentious battle in 1973 to become the first woman member of the House Armed Services Committee, she wasn't given her own seat at the first hearing. She told me that for two years, she and the first African American member of the committee, Ron Dellums (D-CA), found one seat set out for the two of them. One or the other would have to pull up a second chair. The chairman of the committee, F. Edward Hebert (D-LA), proclaimed, "That girl and that black are each worth about half. I'll give them one chair."[1]

And, although Pat authored and introduced the Family and Medical Leave Act, she was relegated to being in the audience at the White House bill signing.

She taught me how to try to take everything in stride, and that it was much more important to accomplish something, even if others stole the credit, than to worry about getting credit yourself. She taught me a lot about the art of debating. She also taught me how to laugh when things happened that made me want to either laugh or cry.

I'll never forget one of my favorite Schroeder moments: On the House floor, members refer to each other as the "gentleman from Kentucky" or the "gentlelady from California." One day, when an opposing member was being exceedingly nasty in a floor debate, Pat requested a point of order— a clarification of rules by the presiding officer. She asked the chair whether she had to call her opponent a "gentleman even if he's not."

I'll never match Pat's oratorical skills or her clever sense of humor. But she was an inspiration to me as I worked to find my own voice on the daunting stage that is the US House of Representatives.

Mentors and role models can do so much to change the way women and girls view themselves and their potential. Day in and day out, women need to do a better job of acting as mentors and seeking them out for ourselves. We also need to urge the men in our lives and at our workplaces to mentor women and girls so they will realize their full potential.

BARTLEBY, THE SBA

In their book *What Women Really Want*, pollsters Celinda Lake and Kellyanne Conway cheered female entrepreneurs, breathlessly declaring: "Women are looking at the culture of work in America and saying, 'We can do better.' Instead of rushing to join the rat race and elbowing their way to the top of the frenzied pack, women are engineering a new work mode in entrepreneurial ventures and nontraditional environments."

When I read that, I wished I felt like cheering, too. I think it's wonderful

For Californian Pam Feder, "small-business owner" was merely a glorified term for just scraping by. Pam and her husband had split up when their daughter, Ashley, was five. Pam, who had a college degree and previous experience as an advertising salesperson, had opted to be a stay-at-home mom after Ashley was born. After the separation, she couldn't find a job that would allow her to be at home for Ashley before and after school. Determined to keep her daughter out of child care, Pam instead launched a "small business," buying muffins and sandwiches at Costco, wrapping them in plastic wrap, and selling them from a cart to office workers at three Los Angeles high-rises. When Ashley was sick and couldn't go to school, she joined the muffins and sandwiches on the cart. "I was willing to do anything to earn enough money just to make ends meet," Pam told me.

To gain the flexibility she needed, Pam had to launch a "small business" that provided low pay, no benefits, and no intellectual stimulation and "felt demeaning at times."

But by pinching pennies, holding garage sales of her neighbors' belongings, taking other odd jobs, and being remarkably resourceful, she found a way to be with Ashley before and after school, put her through private school on a partial scholarship, and send her off to Brandeis University. Today Ashley attends law school and is an aspiring Supreme Court justice.

Hats off to Pam for doing motherhood the hard way in an American workplace that isn't making women's lives any easier.

when a woman starts her own business if that's her passion, and I hope every woman entrepreneur will be as successful as Oprah.

But I heaved a heavy sigh instead. I know that many women who leave their jobs to start their own businesses aren't celebrating. They're giving up on a workplace that isn't meeting their needs.

I also know that the nation's largest buyer of small-business services— Uncle Sam—has been anything but friendly to women-owned businesses. In 2000, Congress passed a law requiring that the US Small Business Administration (SBA) award a minimum of 5 percent of government contracts to women-owned businesses; this paltry number would be a moderate improvement over the 3 percent that today actually do go to women. Apparently, though, 5 percent of the pie is too much for the Bush administration.

The SBA has taken a "Bartleby, the Scrivener" approach to enforcing the law. Bartleby is the title character of a Herman Melville short story. One day, when Bartleby was asked by his boss to complete a routine assignment, he replied, "I would prefer not to." To every subsequent request, Bartleby answered, "I would prefer not to."

Five percent is the law, and the SBA is mandated to implement it. But it would prefer not to, so it doesn't. The US Women's Chamber of Commerce filed a claim against the SBA for failure to implement the program. In September 2005, a US district court issued an opinion concluding that the delay was "unreasonable" and that the SBA had sabotaged the implementation of the program. Unbelieveably, as of October 2007, the SBA still hadn't implemented the program.

Bartleby was eventually imprisoned. At the SBA, he would have been promoted.

- Women start small businesses at four times the rate of men.[2]

- Women-owned businesses employ 19 million workers and generate $2.5 trillion in sales.[3]

- In a study of 100 business owners, the wage gap between women and men was found to be a staggering 49 cents to a man's dollar,[4] compared to 77 cents to a man's dollar for women working full-time for others.

- According to the US Women's Chamber of Commerce, 48 percent of women-owned businesses generate less than $10,000 in revenue annually; 87 percent produce less than $100,000.[5]

WHERE ARE ALL THE WOMEN ENGINEERS?

When my daughter Virginia, who had excelled in math in high school, was applying for admission to Princeton, she indicated that she intended to continue taking math courses in college.

"Math taught at Princeton is much more advanced," my husband, Clif, told her, suggesting that she would be in over her head. Better to pursue other subjects, he suggested.

Not one who likes to be told what she can't do, Virginia strenuously objected. But Clif tried to insist.

"Oh, my God," I thought as I listened. "He doesn't think she can hack Princeton math. I'm married to Larry Summers."

You probably know that what former Harvard University president Larry Summers lacked in discretion, he made up for in guts when he suggested in January 2005 that innate differences between the abilities of the sexes might result in fewer female mathematicians, scientists, and engineers at top universities and fewer successful women in those fields outside academia. You also probably know that that was the beginning of the end for him at Harvard. Years earlier, I got to know Larry Summers while I worked on the congressional Joint Economic Committee, and he's a brilliant economist. He might have a penchant for sticking his foot in his mouth, but he was a great secretary of the Treasury.

My husband is a *great* guy. He's been wonderfully supportive of our daughters. But he believes Larry Summers was a victim of overzealous political correctness, while I believe my husband and Larry Summers are mired in long-held stereotypes about women and girls in math and science.

The difficulty women have breaking in to math, science, and engineering has always been a legitimate gender-equity issue, but recently the stakes have gotten even higher. Today, the shortage of women in these fields has relevance for the urgent issues of the United States' economic competitiveness and national security.

In the past, this country's leadership in the research and applied sciences of math, science, and engineering helped us win the cold war, lead the world in technological innovation, and become what is today the world's only economic and military superpower.

But we won't be making full use of our capacity for innovation and creativity if women continue to be excluded from these fields. In the fiercely competitive global economy of the 21st century, that will cost America dearly.

More and more, young women and girls tend to be the best-educated members of the workforce. More girls than boys hold student government positions, and in 2005, 66 percent of the students included in *Who's Who Among American High School Students* were girls. At the end of the 1990s, a third more women than men were receiving bachelor's degrees. The US Department of Education suggests that disparity is still increasing.[6]

While we are producing more educated women than men, we are producing nowhere near enough women scientists, mathematicians, and engineers.

Donna Nelson, a tenured chemistry professor at the University of Oklahoma, conducted a study of the top 50 research institutions to see how women faculty in the sciences and engineering are doing. "We have more women getting [bachelor's] degrees in chemistry than men. The problem isn't that women aren't testing the field," she told me. "The prob-

In 2005, I had *breakfast with one of the greatest living role models for women in science, Eileen Collins, who six years earlier had made history by being the first woman to command a space shuttle mission.*

Some colleagues and I had passed a resolution recognizing Collins, mission specialist Wendy Lawrence, and other women who had worked on the most recent mission, a trip by the shuttle Discovery. The mission took particular courage because it was the first shuttle flight since the space shuttle Columbia had broken apart during reentry to Earth's atmosphere in 2003.

Born in 1956, Collins grew up in a lower-middle-class household in upstate New York. Among other minimum wage jobs, she worked as a high school janitor to earn money to take flying lessons. In 1990, she joined NASA. She worked her way up and made history in 1999, when she first commanded a successful shuttle mission.

Eileen retired from NASA in 2006. Today, she speaks throughout the country, urging young women and girls to enter nontraditional fields. "The thing I liked about the NASA culture is that as a woman, I don't feel like I'm any different. NASA would love to hire more women," she told me. "It's a darn shame that there aren't more women out there who have technical degrees."

Though she is sure to "talk to boys and girls" (she is deeply concerned about our country's overall lack of engineers and scientists), she's also proud to be a role model for young women and girls. "I think just by me being there, being a woman, it kind of speaks for itself."

And what a powerful message it is!

lem is that we can't keep them in there … I would say 10, 15 years ago, a lot of women were applying for faculty positions. What the women of today are all saying—and I assume they know—[when] they look at the fields of science, it's not an inviting climate."

Cynthia Friend, the first and until 2005 the only female tenured chemistry professor in Harvard's 371-year history, agrees. She told me she believes science departments are behind the times culturally: "The system doesn't allow people to pursue their different interests. Young people now want to explore more. There should be more opportunity to reenter the system at different points…. We're losing some of our best minds and most creative minds by being so insistent on a narrow career path and conservative."

Friend hopes to see the faculty gender gap narrow and also refers to the need for role models. As my husband and her institution's ex-president both prove, the role models must be women *and* men.

- The number of women who chose math and computer science careers fell by 4 percent between 1993 and 1999.[7]

- Among the undergraduate population at the top 50 research institutions, women are:

    - 13 percent of electrical engineering students
    - 21 percent of physics students
    - 28 percent of computer science students[8]

- The number of women who earn PhDs in science and engineering fields has increased significantly since the 1980s, but they still make up only:

    - 10 percent of mechanical engineering PhDs
    - 13 percent of physics PhDs
    - 27 percent of math PhDs

- The percentages of women with BS degrees in these fields are much higher.

- Women are dramatically underrepresented on university faculties, where they represent just 8 percent of math professors and 12 percent of chemistry professors.

- On the bright side, nearly half of all undergraduates in math and chemistry courses now are women.

WRESTLING *WITH* WOMEN'S SPORTS

Both of my daughters are exceptional athletes. Each was captain of her cross-country team in high school. Christina rowed varsity crew in college. Their proud father once said to me, "Where did they get all this talent? You weren't a good athlete growing up."

"Clif," I reminded him, "I didn't play sports in high school because there *weren't* any sports in high school for girls to play."

Things began to change in 1972, after the passage of Title IX. This important civil rights legislation guaranteed female students equal opportunities in all facets of education, including sports. Title IX established a framework for women to make significant academic, social, professional, and athletic gains.

By 1997, when I attended a major conference on women's leadership, the change was palpable. Women represented a critical mass of doctors, attorneys, and corporate managers, which had hardly been imaginable in 1972.

As I listened to the speakers, each a star in her own field, I was struck by a common thread—almost all of them had played college sports.

It makes sense.

Learning how to win and lose, and how to achieve by giving blood, sweat, and tears, is a critical part of success in every field of pursuit. The business world in particular is all about competition.

Girls of my generation were taught deference and modesty. It was a mind-set that even someone with a competitive streak like me—if I get 85 percent of the vote, I wonder why I didn't get the remaining 15—needed years to overcome.

Athletic competition fosters self-esteem. It helps teach girls and young women not to define their self-worth based on what boys think of them.

Almost everyone agrees that Title IX is almost single-handedly responsible for the revolution in women's sports. But there are some who would like to gut Title IX's equal-access-to-sports provisions.

I met women's soccer icon Mia Hamm in 1999, after the US Women's Soccer Team was honored at the White House for their victory in the World Cup. We flew together to Cape Canaveral in Florida on an Air Force plane with then First Lady Hillary Rodham Clinton to watch the space shuttle Columbia lift off under the command of Eileen Collins.

I caught up with Mia again in 2005 and asked her what differences she saw in today's girls compared to when she was growing up in the 1970s and '80s. "What I see in young girls is greater confidence in themselves," she told me. "They have role models to look up to, and they don't feel as if they have to apologize for being successful, for stepping on someone's toes, for saying, 'Hey, listen, I want to be the best.'"

Mia emphasized that the things girls learn on the playing field are useful far beyond it. Teamwork, responsibility to others, individual performance as part of achieving a team goal, communication, managing high-pressure situations, and even time management, all important parts of team sports, are also vital skills for life.

Since Title IX passed, advocates for minor men's sports programs discontinued by universities have blamed it on the girls. The National Wrestling Coaches Association tried unsuccessfully to take their case alleging that Title IX had resulted in the elimination of "hundreds of men's sports teams" to the Supreme Court. Former Speaker of the House Dennis Hastert (R-IL) grumbled about the "unintended consequences of Title IX."

But the truth is that even today, when it comes to college sports budgets and participants, women still lag behind men. Title IX isn't leading to the demise of minor sports programs; at many schools, male athletic slots are consumed by football in huge numbers. The University of Nebraska had 126 players on its football roster in 2007. If the team were cut down to, say, 100 players—which would still leave dozens of reserve players—26 slots would be available for participants in other sports. If I were a wrestler, I'd stop picking on the women's softball team and go ask the football coach why he needs half the student body standing on his sideline.

The Commission on Opportunity in Athletics was convened by Secretary of Education Rod Paige during President Bush's first term to look at Title IX. It considered a different solution.

At the administration's urging, the commission explored the idea of allowing schools to cut women's sports programs based on e-mail surveys. If enough young women didn't express interest in playing a sport in response to a mass e-mailing, the school could cut that team. The same burden would not be placed on men's teams, since only women would be surveyed about women's sports programs. That tactic revealed a glaring double standard: Men's interest in participating in sports was taken for granted; women's had to be proven.

Opponents of this proposed "clarification to Title IX guidelines" quashed the idea, and after the commission issued its report recommending against the rule's institution in 2004, President Bush pledged to keep the existing guidelines in place.

Then, in March 2005, the policy was simply enacted. It was announced on the Department of Education's Web site on a Friday (the worst news day) when Congress was not in session. Just like that—and despite the commission's recommendation against it—it was put in place.

Former Olympic swimmer Donna de Varona, a member of the commission, was floored. "They just circumvented the process," she told me. "That bothers me more than anything. It was done without congressional oversight or public review or anything that we like to do when we change laws, which is the democratic way."

Fortunately, so far the NCAA—the National Collegiate Athletic Association, the voluntary governing body for collegiate sports programs—has refused to enforce the "clarification." But its resistance could easily be challenged in court.

• Women make up 42 percent of college athletes.[9]

• Women's sports programs receive 36 percent of collegiate athletic budgets.[10]

• Women's sports programs receive 32 percent of collegiate recruiting budgets.[11]

• Girls who play sports are:

  • less likely to take drugs

  • less likely to get pregnant while in their teens

  • more likely to stay in school[12]

STAY-AT-HOME PAY

Remember the dilemma I faced when my first daughter, Christina, was born? My husband calculated that my job wasn't adding to the Maloney coffer, it was cutting into it.

It wasn't just the expenses of working outside the home—child care, commuting, a wardrobe for the workplace—or the additional inevitable expenses—housecleaning services, lunches at work, prepared meals because there's no time to cook.

There was also what University of Southern California professor Edward McCaffery has dubbed the income tax code's "second-earner" bias. By this, McCaffrey means the effectively much higher rate a family's secondary breadwinner (more often than not a woman) is charged. For some families, this bias serves as a disincentive for a wife to hold onto—or take—a job.

Here's how it works: Suppose you have a middle-class family—husband, wife, and two kids—living in New York City. Because the city's cost of living is high, wages are somewhat higher, so he makes $60,000 and she makes $25,000. They file a joint tax return (in most cases, a married couple filing a joint return will pay less income tax than if they filed separately). The husband's first $7,500 of income is taxed at 10 percent by the federal government. His wages between $7,550 and $30,650 are taxed at 15 percent, and upward from there. After taking the standard deduction and child tax credits, the husband's overall effective federal tax rate comes to 7 percent of his gross income.

But the wife's effective tax rate doesn't start at zero, as his did. It starts where the husband's taxable income leaves off—at $60,000. This means that her income is taxed at the 25 percent rate. I'll spare you the math, but the bottom line is that after deductions and credits, her effective federal tax rate is 16 percent of her income.

The same second-earner bias applies to state and local taxes. When you add it all up—federal, state, local, and payroll taxes—the husband's effective tax rate is 21 percent and the wife's is 35 percent.

Alan Dlugash, an accountant in New York City, told me he frequently sees couples for whom a second earner's income is a net loss. "It's clear that a lot of them are fighting with the fact that if they earn $30,000 or $40,000, they're going to lose money," he told me.

Ironically, for practical purposes, low-income people face the worst second-earner penalty of all. As their income grows, they become ineligible for government subsidies such as low-cost housing and Medicaid and for tax benefits like the earned income tax credit.

The result is that too many families cannot live on one income, yet they get little added value from having a second earner in the workforce. When women decide not to take a job for this reason, it exacerbates their overall underutilization in the workforce.

TRICKLE DOWN DRYING UP

What people "make" isn't limited to just their salaries. We all know that it's not what you make; it's what you take home. But what many people fail to factor in is what taxpayers get back from their government by way of benefits. Tax policy and its effects on benefits is one of those broader issues that's really a woman's issue, but it is rarely recognized as such.

As a politician, almost by nature, I *love* to vote for tax cuts. No one has ever walked up to me on the street and berated me for voting to cut their taxes. I can't say the opposite is true.

But other than reducing the marriage penalty, I opposed all of President Bush's tax cuts. They were simply unconscionable.

I voted against them for three reasons. One, they were regressive. Two, they made the federal deficit explode. And three, they expanded the portion of the federal taxes derived from earned income as opposed to unearned income. All three of these measures are disadvantageous for women.

Women's paychecks on average are smaller than men's. Thus, regressive tax cuts disproportionately benefit men. Since women make less money, live longer, and are more likely to be primary caregivers for a child or an elderly parent, they rely more on federal programs that provide nutrition, health care, housing, and home heating assistance as well as on subsidized child care, student loan, and early education programs. Any tax cuts that grow the federal deficit and thus subject social programs to budget cuts, short term or long term, hurt women more than men. Shifting the tax burden from unearned income—such as dividends and capital gains—to earned income hits women hardest because women hold fewer securities and have less unearned income.

President Bush's tax cuts were based on the concept of "trickle-down economics," a policy promoted by Ronald Reagan. The theory is that substantially cutting taxes on high-income people will increase investment and entrepreneurship, which will "trickle down" to middle-class and low-income people in the form of better jobs and higher wages. In theory, this would allow the federal government to keep tax revenues steady even while charging higher-income taxpayers lower tax rates. In other words, the tax cuts would pay for themselves.

Sounds great. If only it worked. Tax cuts generate economic growth, but most of them don't pay for themselves. Under President Reagan, the national debt increased from $1 trillion to almost $3 trillion. We started to pay down the debt under President Clinton, but thanks to President Bush's reckless tax cuts in a time of war, we just passed the $9 trillion mark.

In reality, the theory, as President Bush advanced it, might have been worse than a misjudgment. At its core, it might have been the most sinister and destructive economic strategy in American history, one having an unthinkable cost for women and children. Grover Norquist, president of Americans for Tax Reform, has proudly spoken of draining government's "lifeblood"—tax revenues, in other words. His goal is "to cut government in half in 25 years, to get it down to the size where we can drown it in the bathtub." Charming. Unfortunately, Norquist isn't just a radical antitax activist. He has been described as the "chief architect of President Bush's tax plan."[13] As *New York Times* columnist Paul Krugman noted, President Bush himself "called the disappearing surplus 'incredibly positive news' because it would put Congress in a 'fiscal straitjacket.'"

This mentality proves that those who designed the tax cuts know that trickle-down economics doesn't work. Instead, their feel-good, everybody-benefits rationale is *deliberately designed to fail*. As the deficit spins out of control, the only option will be to raise taxes (which is extremely difficult

Tax revenue shortfalls inspired one man's powerful form of activism. A concerned private citizen, Seymour Durst, installed an electronic scoreboard in Midtown Manhattan that displays the national debt, and each individual's share of it, in real time. I used to cringe every time I went by it.

For a while, the numbers on the debt scoreboard were going down. But now that President Bush has squandered our surplus, Congress is back in a fiscal straitjacket. The numbers on that scoreboard are rising, and I'm cringing all over again.

As of November 24, 2007, the scoreboard pegged the national debt at $9,124,455,661,638.95; you and I each owed $30,051.53. The total debt was rising at a rate of $17,013.88 per second.

in this day and age) or to destroy government programs that disproportionately benefit women.

In the near term, the country's financial problems make it hard to
invest in woman-friendly initiatives like my expanded child-care deduction
or Representative Lynn Woolsey's Family and Workplace Balancing Act.

Even if we had more money, President Bush doesn't share these priorities, and he can veto legislation through 2008. Still, we can continue to
build support for a woman-friendly agenda; pass some short-term measures, such as expanding the Family and Medical Leave Act, which costs
the government nothing; and strengthen our coalition for the future.

- All told, 36 percent of President Bush's tax cuts will go to the top 1
percent of taxpayers in terms of income.[14]

- By one estimate, in 2010, 51.8 percent of President Bush's tax cuts will
go to families whose average family income is about $1.5 million—with
only 17 percent going to 60 percent of America's families with the lowest
income.

- To help offset the cost of tax cuts in 2006:[15]

  - The funds allocated for student loans were cut by a record
    amount. (The Democratic Congress in 2007 was able to miti-
    gate the impact by passing a law that cut fees lenders could
    charge on student loans.)

  - Medicaid cuts were imposed that will force the program to
    charge its beneficiaries—the poor—$10.1 billion in addi-
    tional fees for basic services over 10 years.

  - Child care cuts were imposed that will deny care for 255,000
    children over the same period.

  - Child-support payment enforcement was cut in a way that will
    cost needy families $8.4 billion in unrecovered payments.

SOCIAL SECURITY:
MONEY-BACK GUARANTEE (FOR MEN)

The goal of every family with children is to raise happy, well-adjusted kids. This requires parents to earn enough money to provide the necessities of life and devote significant time to educating and encouraging their children. Parents must divide their time between paid and unpaid work, the lion's share of the latter consisting of caring for children or elderly parents. Statistically, fathers tend to do more paid work while mothers do more unpaid work.[16]

The political right, in particular, champions stay-at-home motherhood. But when it comes down to dollars and cents for retirement, stay-at-

There are good ideas and bad ideas. And then there was former Congressman Bill Thomas's idea for reforming Social Security.

Representative Thomas (R-CA) proposed that since women live longer and therefore receive Social Security benefits for a longer period of time, the annual benefit for women should be cut.

After Congressman Thomas floated this idea on Meet the Press, Congressman Frank Pallone (D-NJ) and I co-wrote President Bush a letter signed by 41 members of Congress. "Congressman Thomas' proposal attacks the most vulnerable among us. Retired women workers are twice as likely [as] men to live below the poverty line and to depend on Social Security as their sole means of support," we wrote.

Luckily, the idea was too wacky for even the Bushies. We haven't heard about it since.

home motherhood is barely valued at all. That's why Ann Crittenden, a former *New York Times* economics reporter and author of *The Price of Motherhood*, calls motherhood "the single biggest risk factor for poverty in old age."

Married couples who stay married receive Social Security benefits in one of two ways. If one spouse accrues less than twice the Social Security benefits of the other, each of them receives the benefit that was earned individually. But if one spouse earns *more* than twice the Social Security benefits of the other spouse, the couple receives the "spousal benefit"—the higher-earning spouse's benefit plus another 50 percent of that benefit. This additional 50 percent is meant to compensate the secondary bread-winner for unpaid caretaking.

But in cases of divorce, the picture is dramatically different. If a couple divorces after less than 10 years of marriage, each spouse gets only the benefits he or she earned in the paid workforce. If you're a stay-at-home mom taking care of, say, three children, and you and your husband divorce after 9 years of marriage, although your husband is still entitled to receive his full Social Security benefit, you are not eligible for benefits based on his earnings!

If you're a stay-at-home mom who gets divorced after more than 10 years of marriage, your financial outcome will be better. At retirement, you will have access to the same spousal benefit—50 percent of his entitlement—that you would have received if you hadn't divorced. Here's the catch: If your ex-husband dies, you are entitled to 100 percent of his annual benefit; in the eyes of the Social Security Administration, he's worth twice as much dead as alive. That might qualify as a motive in a murder mystery.

This Social Security formula is a particularly bitter pill for women to swallow because women generally are more reliant on Social Security than men are.[17] Since women tend to make less money over the course of their careers, they end up with smaller pensions and less investment income. And, since women's life expectancy is four years longer than men's, their retirements tend to be longer and more expensive. As they get older, their savings dwindle, and they depend more on Social Security.

To correct the most glaring injustice, I've introduced a bill that would make the spousal benefit available after 5 years of marriage instead of 10.

• In 2004, median retirement income—which combines Social Security benefits, pensions, and income from savings and investments—was $21,102 for men and $12,020 for women.[18]

• Women's average annual Social Security benefit was $3,156 less than men's.[19]

AN ERA FOR THE ERA

Some of the battles talked about in this book would be more easily resolved with passage of the Women's Equality Amendment, also known as the Equal Rights Amendment (ERA). This constitutional amendment, passed by Congress in the 1970s but never ratified by the needed three-quarters of states to make it federal law, would guarantee equal rights and equal protection under the law for women.

Though women have a patchwork of legal protections today—the Equal Protection Clause, Title VII, Title IX, the Equal Pay Act, the Pregnancy Discrimination Act, the Violence against Women Act, and others—the reality is that prohibitions against sex discrimination are not as strongly enforceable as prohibitions against race discrimination. Other than the Equal Protection Clause (part of the Constitution's 14th Amendment), these protections at the state level could be wiped away by Congress with a simple majority vote. Even worse, as we've seen, the protections can be gutted by totally undemocratic "administrative actions" taken by the executive branch (see "Wrestling *with* Women's Sports"

The Equal Rights Amendment *(which is also called the Women's Equality Amendment) should have passed generations ago. The first Woman's Rights Convention, in 1848 in Seneca Falls, New York, sparked a movement that would eventually give rise to the modern feminist movement and the drive to pass the ERA. Led by Susan B. Anthony, Lucretia Mott, and Elizabeth Cady Stanton, one of the suffragists' primary goals was to win the right to vote. That was finally achieved in 1920, after decades of activism during which founder Alice Paul and members of her National Woman's Party were attacked, arrested, imprisoned, institutionalized, and force-fed—all of which only inspired more support for their cause.*

Three years later, in 1923, Paul drafted the language of the ERA. But it wasn't until 1972 that the ERA actually passed both houses of Congress and went to the states for ratification. Thirty-eight state legislatures—three-fourths of the total—had to vote yes within 10 years to have the provision appended to the Constitution. By the time of the deadline in 1982, only 35 had done so.

on page 64). Finally, unfriendly courts—today's Supreme Court comes to mind—can rule in ways that overturn long-standing tradition and precedent.

If we passed the Women's Equality Amendment, legislators and judges would have to equitably take into account women's experiences when considering making changes to Social Security, taxes, wages, pensions, domestic relations, insurance, and more. Actuarial tables like those initially used to determine benefits under the Victim Compensation Fund provisions after 9/11 would be unconstitutional. Mothers would have protection against employment discrimination based on their parental roles. Fathers would get a boost in family court, where many men feel they are at a disadvantage in custody battles.

The Women's Equality Amendment would allow advocates, other legislators, and me to stop playing the role of the proverbial "little Dutch boy" (make that "little Dutch girl"), employing stopgap measures to grant equality that should be constitutionally guaranteed. So much of what I have done in recent years has amounted to running around trying to plug holes in a patchwork levee that is under enormous pressure. I want to make progress for women, not just defend it.

We need constitutional rights, not legislative fights. As it stands now, what judges and lawmakers giveth, they can also taketh away.

Opponents argue that this fight has already been fought, and women's equality lost. The myth they would have us believe is that Phyllis Schlafly defeated the ERA by leading in protest masses of women who feared losing the right to be supported by their husbands.

According to my good friend Feminist Majority Foundation president Eleanor Smeal, this is simply not true. Rallies of ERA supporters, she asserts, vastly outnumbered those of opponents.

Ellie, who worked tirelessly on the ERA campaign in states all around the country, told me that the ERA wasn't lost in the public square; it was lost behind closed doors. It wasn't lost over principles, she explained. It was defeated with cold, hard cash.

Insurance companies, banks, and other corporate interests thought the amendment would be bad for business. Insurance companies would no longer be able to charge women higher health insurance premiums, deny pregnancy coverage, or pay out less on women's annuity plans because of their longer lifespan. Banks would have to give credit to women on an equal basis.

States' rights advocates played a smaller role. They saw the ERA as a federal power grab and preferred to preserve their right to discriminate.

Over the years, 21 states have passed their own versions of the ERA. I submitted testimony in support of a proposal for a New York ERA at a hearing before the New York State legislature as recently as 2004.

On the federal level, I have sponsored the Women's Equality Amendment during every congressional term since 1997. With many others, I have built a base of support whose strength is indicated by the bill's 202 cosponsors (as of November 2007).

But don't count on automatic support from Democrats. For the first time since the Women's Equality Amendment was introduced as the ERA, the Democratic Party left the proposal out of its platform in 2004.

We need to lean on our federal legislators to make the Women's Equality Amendment a priority. I believe it would pass by a wide margin if it came to a full vote in Congress.

One school of thought says the Women's Equality Amendment would be etched into the Constitution if three additional states were to ratify it. The Madison Amendment, a constitutional amendment concerning congressional pay raises that was introduced in 1789 but not ratified by three-fourths of the states until 1992, may have established a precedent for an open-ended ratification period that would support the so-called three-state strategy for enacting the Women's Equality Amendment. Representative Rob Andrews (D-NJ) has introduced legislation to implement the three-state strategy.

Whether that line of reasoning would pass muster with the courts is an open question, especially since a few states have tried to *rescind* their ratification.

We may still reach our 38-state goal, however. In 2003, a Florida State Senate committee approved a measure to ratify the amendment. That same year, the Illinois House of Representatives voted nearly two to one in favor of the Women's Equality Amendment. There have also been positive rumblings in Missouri.

Still, the surest way is to start over in Congress while also working on the three-state strategy on a parallel track.

We have a lot of work to do, but the dream lives on. The legacy that I would like to leave is an impenetrable levee that shores up women's equality for good—a wall so impervious to attacks on equality that it cannot be torn down. A wall that ends the need for little Dutch girls to run around plugging holes and lets me die in peace. A wall that allows Susan B.

What does the Women's Equality Amendment—all 52 words of it—actually say?

"Equality of rights under the law shall not be denied or abridged by the United States or by any state on account of sex. The Congress shall have the power to enforce, by appropriate legislation, the provisions of this article. This amendment shall take effect two years after the date of ratification."

Anthony, Elizabeth Cady Stanton, Lucretia Mott, and Alice Paul to stop rolling in their graves.

That sanctified wall is the Women's Equality Amendment.

Ladies and like-minded gentlemen, put up that wall!

• A 2001 survey showed that more than 9 of every 10 people think men and women should have equally protected rights.

• More than 7 in 10 people erroneously believe it is already guaranteed.[20]

Take-Action Guide

Equal Opportunity for All

1. Battle the stereotypes that hold women back.

Get a Catalyst report into the hands of those who run
your organization and its management training programs.
Spread the word on how stereotypes work so others can make
the subconscious conscious. Go to www.catalyst.org/files.

2. Promote parity for women-owned and women-run businesses.

• **Buy from women-owned and women-run businesses.**
The National Association for Female Executives lists the top
30 companies for female executives at www.nafeonline.com/
web?service=direct/1/ViewArticlePage/dlinkFullArticle&sp=
S257&sp=245. Women's Business Enterprise National Council
(www.wbenc.org) has information on women-owned businesses
to help you decide whom to support with your dollars.

• **Start your own small business.** A number of resources
are available for women who are considering starting their
own businesses. Two good places to begin are www.womanowned.
com and the US Women's Chamber of Commerce
(www.uswcc.org).

• **If you already own a business, make use of the resources
available to you.** The US Women's Chamber of Commerce
lists female contractors and provides small-business loans for

women entrepreneurs; be sure that your company is listed and you have access to their programs by checking www.uswcc.org/ guide.

3. Help girls and young women thrive at playing sports.

• **Play sports with your kids.** There's no better way to encourage your daughter to play sports than to play with her. The Women's Sports Foundation has tips on encouraging and nurturing young athletes at www.womenssportsfoundation.org. To get more involved, call your local school, Little League, or other kids' sports organization and find out whether they need assistant or head coaches. Find local volunteer opportunities at www.gogirlgonetwork.org.

• **Cheer.** Regularly take your sons and daughters to sporting events at any level. Buy season tickets to female professional and college games. Take a Kid to the Game (www.takg.com) sells discounted NCAA tickets for children.

• **Sponsor a girl athlete or a girls' team.** The Women's Sports Foundation's GoGirlGo! Network (www.gogirlgonetwork.org) and the Mia Hamm Foundation (www.miafoundation.org) both offer opportunities.

• **Protect Title IX.** Keep abreast of federal and legislative issues at www.titleix.info, which is sponsored by the MARGARET Fund of the National Women's Law Center. Click on the Take Action link to send a message telling the Department of Education secretary what you think. Start by registering your opposition to the Title IX "clarification" by selecting Access to Higher Education. Write to your federal legislators as well. The

American Association of University Women has posted a series of comprehensive Title IX position papers at www.aauw.org/ issue_advocacy/actionpages/index.cfm, and their Two-Minute Activist page, http://capwiz.com/aauw/home, makes being heard about important legislative issues as simple as clicking a mouse.

4. Help women meet America's critical need for mathematicians and scientists.

• **Encourage universities and schools to address gender inequities and attract women instructors to act as role models.** If you are in college or have children in college, check to be sure that the university follows hiring and tenure guidelines that do not discriminate against women. The MIT Gender Equity Project grew out of one courageous woman professor's successful battle against discrimination. Go to http://web.mit.edu/gep/about. html#committees to learn how to apply its findings and approaches at other schools.

• **Work with trade organizations** that offer networking, mentoring, and training opportunities for women and girls interested in math and science. The Association for Women in Science (www.awis.org) researches and works to combat bias against women in science, provides updates on policy issues (www.awis.org/pubs/wire.html), and offers mentoring and networking opportunities. The Association for Women in Mathematics (www.awm-math.org) has a mentoring program for women developing careers in mathematics. The Society of Women Engineers (www.swe.org) offers Web seminars, leadership conferences, and loads of information for everyone from kindergarteners to professionals. WITI, founded as the International Network of Women in Technology (www.witi.com), is an international trade association for women in technology that has networks for professionals, executives, students, and others.

5. Fight for progressive tax reform that benefits women.

• **Do not support tax cuts without knowing what—and whom— they will hurt.** The Center on Budget and Policy Priorities frequently updates their analyses of tax cut proposals and more at www.cbpp.org. Citizens for Tax Justice posts action alerts and policy proposals at www.ctj.org. The National Council for Research on Women's 2006 book *Taxes Are a Women's Issue* goes into much more detail than I can here and is worth every dime it costs. Buy it at www.ncrw.org/publications/taxes.htm.

• **Don't believe the hype!** Many ill-advised policy decisions are sold to the American public using a combination of misrepresentation and media hype. The Council on Contemporary Families looks at the reality behind the hype. Their Web site, www.contemporaryfamilies. org, is well worth checking out.

• **Make sure you get the tax breaks that are due to you.** The National Women's Law Center's Web site, www.nwlc.org/display. cfm?section=tax, has links to information on tax credits and deductions that are often overlooked by women.

• **Support my bill to make all child-care expenses business expenses** so they are eligible for the same 75 percent deduction that can be applied to entertainment at a strip club. Go to my Web site, http:// maloney.house.gov, for more information.

6. Work to make sure Social Security provides security for women.

• **Support my Social Security bill,** which will lower from 10 to 5 the number of years a divorced couple will have had to be married to make the spouse eligible for spousal benefits under Social Security.

• **Educate yourself about Social Security.** Arm yourself with information from the National Women's Law Center at www.nwlc. org/display.cfm?section=social%20security and the American Association of University Women at www.aauw.org/advocacy/ issue_advocacy/actionpages/upload/AAUW-Social-Security-and-Women-110.pdf.

• **Take action.** OWL—the Older Women's League—has developed a Social Security Matters Web site, www.socialsecuritymatters.org, that offers information and opportunities for taking action. AARP has a legislative action page, www.capitolconnect.com/ aarp, that alerts viewers to pending laws that could affect Social Security and other benefits granted to older Americans. The Women's Institute for a Secure Retirement has fact sheets and tips galore on starting to secure your own financial future, available at www.wiserwomen.org.

• **Make equality for women a constitutionally guaranteed right.** The National Council of Women's Organizations' ERA Task Force works to raise interest in and awareness of the ongoing effort to fully ratify the ERA. See www.womensorganizations.org for information and updates. Urge your federal legislators to support a vote on the Women's Equality Amendment. Another organization devoted to passing the amendment, 4era.org, offers news, information, and events at its Web site (http://4tera.org). If you live in Illinois, Florida, Arizona, or Missouri, 4era can use your help with the "three-state strategy" for passing the ERA. You can find more information about the history and current status of the ERA at www.equalrightsamendment.org.

4

HEALTH CARE THAT'S ALWAYS THERE

"Of all the forms of inequality, injustice in health care is the most shocking and inhumane."

—MARTIN LUTHER KING JR.

America has the world's most technologically advanced medical system. At its very best, the system provides extraordinary care. People fly in from all over the world to take advantage of leading-edge technology available at hospitals in my own district, such as the New York University Medical Center, New York-Presbyterian–Cornell Hospital, and Memorial Sloan-Kettering Cancer Center, and to be treated by some of the best doctors in the world. Many of them will pay any price. The quality of care they get speaks to the *potential* of our health-care system.

But the reality for too many people in our country is very different. Our health-care system, the most expensive in the world, is far from the best. Among the industrialized countries, it ranks near the bottom in terms of outcomes, while our fast-growing population of those who lack health insurance ranks first in number.

As with so much else, it is women who disproportionately are on the losing end and suffer the consequences of our two-tiered system.

How has the health-care system gone so badly wrong and wrought such catastrophic consequences? The short answer is that bad policies, flawed "free-market" health insurance, special-interest politics, and the absence of consensus among the American people all contribute.

REAL FAMILY VALUES

There is one issue conservative Republicans and I agree about: Family values matter.

The problem is, we define our terms a little differently.

That's what I learned on April 14, 2005, during debate on the House floor about a bill to stiffen bankruptcy laws. The bill greatly increased the amount of credit card debt that individuals and families would still owe after declaring bankruptcy.

The change was ostensibly focused on thwarting ne'er-do-wells trying to abuse the system. Unfortunately, its real targets were a wide universe of hardworking Americans who had fallen on hard times. These were the very Americans that bankruptcy protection was created to protect.

Among the many individuals who were sure to suffer under the law were those with illnesses whose costs medical insurance—if they had it— wasn't covering and divorced women who were owed child support.

I tried to attach an amendment to the bill that would have put child-support payments ahead of credit card payments in the order of creditors whom fathers would pay first after declaring bankruptcy. Like all of the Democratic amendments proposed that day, it was rejected—it was just another day in the Republican-dominated chamber.

I tried to have submitted into the *Congressional Record* letters from women's groups and others condemning the fact that children were put second behind the credit card companies. "This is wrong," I said. "Where are the family values in this Congress? Is it just rhetoric, or do you really care about children?" Apparently, I hit a nerve.

Congressman Sam Johnson (R-TX) objected to my request to put the letters into the record—an almost unheard-of motion! Submitting third-party letters into the *Congressional Record* is as routine as asking someone to pass the butter at dinner. And Congressman Phil Gingrey (R-GA) had just submitted letters.

But in Johnson's mind, I hadn't made a routine request. I had committed what amounted to a trademark violation. The message was clear: Republicans hold a monopoly on "family values."

My Democratic colleagues were just as surprised as I was. Three of them—Alcee Hastings (FL), Jerrold Nadler (NY), and Maxine Waters (CA)—went to bat for me. In an almost comical exchange, they barraged the member presiding over the debate with questions about arcane parliamentary procedure.

After much ado about nothing, the letters found their way into the *Congressional Record*. But the whole escapade illustrated the other side's lack of sensitivity when it comes to discussion of *real* family values.

President Bush and some of his Republican allies in Congress were stunningly insensitive to the health-care needs of children whose parents can't afford health insurance.

In 2007, Democrats in the House and Senate, with some support from

Republican members, passed a bill to continue and expand the State Children's Health Insurance Program (SCHIP) to cover an additional four million children.[1]

President Bush vetoed the bill, citing a sudden, seemingly unprecedented attack of fiscal responsibility! What brings out the stinginess in a man who exploded the deficit with unprecedented tax cuts in the middle of a war? The "family value" of helping families, often led by single mothers, obtain health care for their children.

The waning of affordable and available health care is very much a woman's issue, though it often goes unrecognized as such.

Women use the system more—we're the ones who have babies, we have more complex reproductive systems, and we live longer—so our health-care expenses are higher. At the same time, as I've explained, we make less money than men and are less likely to be able to afford health insurance. On top of that, we are more likely than men to be insured under a spouse's plan. That makes us doubly vulnerable in cases of divorce or widowhood.

The average debtor who is bankrupted for medical reasons isn't a slacker high school dropout. It's a 41-year-old woman—a hardworking mother like so many we know; she is a homeowner and attended at least some college.[2]

- At least 46 percent of all bankruptcies originate in the tangled web that is our health-care system.

- Medical-related bankruptcies increased by 2,300 percent between 1981 and 2001.[3]

- Eighty-two million Americans—more than a quarter of the population—go without insurance at some point in any given year, and 46 million have no health insurance at all.[4] Most are one serious illness away from being badgered by collection agencies or having their day in bankruptcy court.

• Three-quarters of people driven into bankruptcy because of illness *did* have health insurance at the onset of their illness but are among the growing number of the "underinsured."[5]

• Two-thirds of those who lost their health insurance in 2004 were women.[6]

• Insured women are twice as likely to get a potentially lifesaving annual Pap test as uninsured women.[7]

• As of 2003, women ages 65 and older made up 57 percent of Medicare beneficiaries; among Medicare beneficiaries 85 and older, 72 percent were women.[8]

• 90 percent of Americans believe the health-care system needs either fundamental changes or a complete overhaul.[9]

IT'S A WOMAN THING

As women search for good health care, there is one hurdle that is not as high as it once was: More and more often, the medical establishment responds to our needs. We've come a long way.

In the process of giving birth to my second daughter, I pushed so hard that my bladder dropped below where it is supposed to be; surgery was required to move it back where it belonged. My doctor recommended that while he was fixing my bladder, it would also be a good idea to remove my ovaries to reduce the possibility of later developing cancer. Naively, I agreed.

I told a friend, journalist Barbara Seaman, that I was planning to have the operation. Barbara is the author of *The Greatest Experiment Ever Performed on Women* and one of our nation's most powerful voices on the health risks of estrogen. She heroically took on the pharmaceutical companies and exposed their suppression of research establishing the dangers of estrogen.

The insurance industry tried to discredit Barbara at every turn, but recent research from the Women's Health Initiative (WHI) supports the

Linda was just a few years from retirement when she was laid off from her job at a factory in her home state of South Carolina. Soon after that, her doctor, Paul DeMarco, began urging her to have a colonoscopy. Although a small amount of blood detected in her stool was worrisome, Linda held off on having the test because it was expensive, and her low-cost health insurance, obtained through AARP, wouldn't cover it.

When she finally had the test, she learned that she had rectal cancer.

The colonoscopy had been a financial setback, but the subsequent surgery, radiation, and chemotherapy were one-way tickets to a lifetime of indentured servitude at the hands of the health-care system. Only a tiny fraction of Linda's hospital stay—eight days total, five in the ICU—was covered by her insurance. "When I left, my hospital bill was close to $50,000," she told me. "And then I had to pay for my radiation."

Fortunately, the McLeod Cancer Center for Treatment and Research in Florence, South Carolina, helped pay for her chemotherapy. But Linda was already deeply in medical debt and getting deeper. As someone who had lived all her life debt-free, the tens of thousands of dollars she owed seemed insurmountable.

arguments she's been making for years. While WHI data found no statistically significant increase in breast cancer risk in postmenopausal women who were on estrogen replacement therapy, it did find dramatically increased risks of strokes and blood clots—so much so that it ended its study prematurely.

Barbara was horrified to learn that I was planning to have my healthy and vital ovaries removed, and she spread the word to dozens of women she knew. "Contact Congresswoman Maloney," she told her friends.

"All these bills—they still keep coming from everywhere," she said. "I got a bill on Saturday and said, 'I don't even recognize that name!'"

She asked Dr. DeMarco whether there were any programs that could help her. "'If I don't get any help, I'll probably be paying this till I die,'" she told him. Linda and her husband rejected the idea of filing for bankruptcy. "It would worry me to death. We just depend on the Lord," she said.

Linda ultimately negotiated an installment plan that will leave her debt-free at age 111.

If Linda had been a little bit poorer, she would have qualified for Medicaid. If she had been a little bit older, she would have qualified for Medicare. If the factory where she worked hadn't laid her off, she would have had employer-provided health coverage. If her husband hadn't retired from his full-time job earlier that year, she would have been covered under his policy.

And if the richest country in the world didn't have a decency deficit, she wouldn't have found herself in financial quicksand—facing a choice between declaring bankruptcy and living in deep debt until she takes her last breath.

"Tell her not to have her ovaries out!" For a week, I was barraged with phone calls from women I didn't know who told me "Don't do it."

If you've ever wondered whether calling elected officials can make them change their minds, you should know that I'm still the proud owner of a pair of ovaries.

I owe a debt of gratitude to Barbara and all the people who called. It turns out the procedure my doctor recommended induces surgical menopause and therefore can cause osteoporosis, cardiovascular disease, and other problems associated with low hormone levels. In 2005, the American College of Obstetricians and Gynecologists changed its recommendations after a study found no long-term benefits to removing healthy ovaries in younger women. As usual, Barbara Seaman was right.

My experience illustrates the historic inequity in research on women's health. Over the last quarter-century, the situation has improved—some.

When she was once asked what everyday difference she was most proud of making while in Congress, former representative Pat Schroeder responded, "When I got there, the research they were doing at the National Institutes of Health had no studies on women; they weren't even using female rats! So we knew zip about women's health. They even did the breast cancer research on men!"

Shortly before I was elected to the House, the Congressional Women's Caucus actually had to pass legislation to ensure that all clinical studies on women's health would be conducted on women. Over time, momentum built for passing the Women's Health Equity Act, which sought to promote greater equity in women's health care through better access to health-care services and more research. It passed during my first term in Congress, along with additional funding for women's health research.

In those first two years, I also worked closely with Congresswoman Barbara Vucanovich (R-NV), a breast cancer survivor, to make inroads for early detection. It's hard to find anyone who hasn't been touched by a disease that strikes one in seven women. When we circulated a letter to President Clinton asking him to include funding in Medicare for annual mammograms in his budget, hundreds of members signed it. It is now law. I wondered what everyone had been waiting for! I later worked with Representative Connie Morella (R-MD) to pass legislation requiring Medicare to cover screening for osteoporosis.

I am very proud of the progress we've made. There are now more female doctors and more funds available for research into women's health issues than when I gave birth or arrived in Congress. But we have much more to do in the fight for women's health.

Emphasizing the prevention of health problems is one of the simplest, cheapest, and most effective solutions. I currently have a bill before Congress that would require insurance companies to cover screening for osteoporosis, breast cancer, prostate cancer, and colorectal cancer. It is one of the most most popular pieces of legislation I'm working on.

And for good reason. One study found that preventable diseases account for 70 percent of our illnesses and our health-care costs.[10] One urgent and prevalent example is cancer. Forty percent of all cancers may be preventable simply with lifestyle changes, and an even higher percentage can be successfully treated if they're detected early.[11] Given that 678,060 US women are diagnosed with cancer every year, and the cost of cancer treatment is approaching $80 billion annually in the United States, the potential that prevention has to save lives and curb the soaring cost of health care is staggering.[12]

The idea that an ounce of prevention is worth a pound of cure appears lost on the Bush administration, however. In a characteristic act of whittling away at women's rights in a way that 99 percent of Americans will never hear about, President Bush proposed a budget cut that would take money away from the National Breast and Cervical Cancer Early Detection Program. The program provides free or low-cost screening to women who otherwise couldn't afford it. At the time he proposed the cut, the

You don't have to occupy the governor's mansion to do great things for women's health. Anna Kril was a volunteer on my first campaign for Congress in the Queens portion of my district. Shortly after I won that race, Anna was diagnosed with breast cancer. On one of my first trips back from Washington, I stopped by the hospital, where she was preparing for a double mastectomy, and gave her a rose. She looked incredibly downcast and told me she felt alone with her illness.

In an effort to get her mind off her situation, I suggested that when she got through with her surgery, she should start the kind of support group that wasn't available to her. She brightened up a bit and said, "Maybe I will."

I often encourage people to work in public service in some capacity. I get a lot of polite smiles. But about six months after I visited Anna in the hospital, I got a call from her.

"I took your advice," she said.

The next year, I was running for reelection in Queens and marching in the Columbus Day parade. Anna Kril and several other women were right behind me, holding a giant banner emblazoned with the name of her new (deliberately misspelled) organization: Astoria Queens SHAREing and CAREing.

Anna's group has since helped thousands of women get through cancer without feeling alone. In addition to holding workshops for breast cancer patients and survivors, SHAREing and CAREing helps women avoid going through what Anna went through by sponsoring mammograms that detect breast cancer before a mastectomy is necessary.

Anna has given women from western Queens a new outlook on life after breast cancer. All I gave Anna was a rose.

program had only enough funding to serve approximately 20 percent of low-income women. In other words, the president wants to cut the program at a time when it should be quintupled!

Another area in which we must improve is the battle against diseases that stem from issues of self-esteem.

A few years ago, my daughter came home from middle school with a Barbie doll.

"Aren't you a little old for that?" I asked her.

"Look at this," she said, pointing to Barbie's waist. "This isn't normal. This isn't how a woman's body is supposed to look."

She was right. If Barbie were 6 feet tall, she would weigh 101 pounds have a 39-inch bust, 33-inch hips, and a 19-inch waist. Disney characters are no better. Ariel, Jasmine, and Pocahontas all sport deep cleavage and waistlines the size of their ankles. Before girls are even out of diapers, they're exposed to mutant role models that can create a perception of a "right" body image that is all wrong.

As they got older, my daughters would come home with something even more upsetting: stories of classmates who were bulimic or anorexic. I didn't even know what bulimia or anorexia were until I was in my late teens. Today, no one goes that long without seeing these conditions up close.

The tyranny of body image today represents an unqualified failure of the women's movement that has taken a terrible toll on the health of young women and girls. Our health-care system has enough problems to deal with without adding the self-inflicted harm of conforming to a dangerous ideal. Meryl Streep told me she thinks promoting this ideal is a way to make women "diminished and less than."

It's almost common knowledge that Hollywood stars have body doubles. "Actors are profoundly vain, but business savvy, too. It's all about selling fantasies," explained Miranda Banks, a film studies professor at the Otis College of Art and Design in Los Angeles.

Here I must make a confession. I too have had a body double. In my first race for Congress, polls showed that support from women would be essential. I had so little money that I couldn't afford to send direct mail to all Democrats in the district, so I just mailed to households with Democratic women.

The advertisement showed the legs of three men in suits in a group, presumably having a conversation. Standing apart from the men was a woman in a skirt. The text said it all: "Some people go to Congress to *have* a job. ... Some people go to Congress to *do* a job." I had been scheduled to pose at the photo shoot, but at the last minute, I had to divert for a campaign stop. One of my staffers, Jeanne Waller, stood in for me. My legs were fine. Jeanne's legs were *spectacular*.

And they were real. I recently read that 85 percent of body doubles' breasts are "enhanced." Girls try to live up to standards that literally aren't even human.

And major procedures like surgery aren't the only concerns. I appeared on NBC's *Today* show in April 2006 to discuss a bill I had introduced along with Representative Ginny Brown-Waite (R-FL) to require the FDA to review its labeling requirements on tanning machines, which substantially understate the risks of irreversible skin damage.

After the show, I received an e-mail from Emily Konesky of Buffalo. Three days after her 19th birthday, Emily was diagnosed with stage three malignant melanoma, which has a 20 percent 10-year survival rate. She had since undergone multiple surgeries. Her single round of chemotherapy was stopped because, as Emily put it, "I would have ended up dying from the chemo instead of the cancer." In an age of disposable correspondence, I will keep Emily's e-mail forever.

Being a normal teenager ... is a very distant memory for me. I can't even remember when I went out with my friends. ... I was also one of those girls that went to a tanning bed every day, religiously worshipping the sun and those stupid cancer boxes. I didn't think it was wrong or bad. Nobody ever told me that melanoma was something that could happen to me. The only warnings I saw in tanning beds were [about] eyewear protection. I actually turned on the radio and heard a commercial the other day for a tanning bed and the first thing the commercial announcer said was "Did you know that tanning in tanning beds is good for you?" I wanted to throw up when I heard that and almost had a breakdown. ... Not enough people know about the dangers of skin cancer. Skin cancer is something that [normally] takes 20 to 30 years to develop. It SHOULDN'T be happening to women in their 20s or 30s ... let alone to a 19-year-old. EVERY HOUR SOMEONE DIES FROM MELANOMA! ... I was given a second chance for a reason, to devote my life to helping people that are dealing with cancer. My boyfriend Mark and I are ready to dedicate our lives to helping others who had been in my same situation and to ensure that this horrible thing will never happen to anyone again. ... So please, if there's any way we could talk, I am willing to drive anywhere, anytime, any distance. ... It would be amazing if I could be part of something that could save thousands and millions of lives.

Emily is the one who is amazing. I gave her a call and before long, she was on Capitol Hill speaking to members of Congress about our bill.

Appearing with Emily was my friend Kate White, the editor-in-chief of *Cosmopolitan*. Kate and her editorial department are conscious of the positive effect that beauty magazines can have on the self-images of women who don't believe they measure up to a beauty "ideal." She told me they will not run dieting stories, that they write about plastic surgery only to point out the risks, and that they believe in giving readers information that will allow them to make smart choices about their health.

As Kate told me, "Our Gen X and Gen Y readers are concerned about their health, and they want information about how to take care of themselves. We like hearing from readers who tell us that our Practice Safe Sun campaign made a difference for them and helped them recognize that tanning and tanning salons can harm them." *Cosmopolitan* was an important part of the campaign to pass my tanning legislation.

It's tragic that just getting girls to eat normally, remain silicon-free, and stay out from under tanning lamps has become a form of preventive health care.

- Up to 1 percent of girls and women suffer from anorexia, and up to 2 percent have bulimia.[13]

- A study by the University of Minnesota found that 20 percent of girls surveyed had used diet pills by age 20.[14]

- The number of girls under the age of 17 who got breast implants rose from about 4,000 to 11,000 between 2002 and 2003.[15]

- The majority of breast implants leak eventually—by one estimate, more than 50 percent of them within just 10 years—and will have to be replaced to reduce the risk of illness and injury.[16]

- Nearly half of all 18- and 19-year-old women have visited a tanning salon at least three times.[17]

- Going under the lamp just once a month increases the risk of melanoma, the deadliest form of skin cancer, by 55 percent.[18]

HUMVEES OR HEALTH CARE?

It's a uniquely American indecency that some people, mostly conservatives, believe that health care isn't a right but rather a set of goods and services available on the free market to those who can afford to pay for them, like cashmere sweaters, publicists, and Humvees.

Rush Limbaugh, conservative talk show host, went so far as to characterize Maryland's 2006 Fair Share Health Care law as "government-sanctioned rape." What connection there is between violent sexual assault and a law that compels large, profitable corporations to provide their workers and their families with minimal medical coverage escapes me. Most Americans believe that medicines, doctor visits, and vaccines should be available to those who can't afford to buy coverage on the open market.

Private insurers are increasingly unwilling to offer essential healthcare policies at prices that are affordable for everyone. Some Americans can't purchase health insurance at *any* price. Applicants have been denied insurance for having varicose veins and attention deficit disorder, or for having briefly seen a psychologist after a divorce.[19] Insurance companies spend a great deal of time and money trying to determine whom not to cover.

In addition to leaving tens of millions of Americans uninsured or underinsured, our system has the world's highest administrative costs *by a mile*. Administrative costs include anything not spent on the care itself: paperwork, marketing, underwriting, and profits. Doctors and hospitals have absurdly high administrative costs as well, due in part to the cost of dealing with the 1,500 individual insurance companies.

• The number of people without health insurance rose to about 16 percent between 2001 and 2005, meaning that the United States has the industrialized world's highest percentage of people who are uninsured.[20]

• We also rank first in cost: In 2004, by one estimate, health care for one person in the United States cost $6,102. Canada, Australia, and Britain spent about half that, or less.[21]

• Despite its high cost, the World Health Organization ranked America's health-care system 37th in the world for outcomes.

• Our life expectancy ranks 42nd—down from 11th just two decades ago.[22]

• Our infant mortality rate ranks 40th, with 6.8 deaths per 1,000 live births.[23]

• Estimates of the overall administrative costs of our health-care system range between 20 and 31 percent.[24]

• Compared to 1970, we have 40 percent more doctors and 3,000 percent more medical administrators today.[25]

LOBBYISTS BEFORE DOCTORS

The insurance lobby was the driving force behind the defeat of the Clinton health-care package during my first term in Congress, as well as the source of the successful and misleading "Harry and Louise" ads.

It was also insurance lobbyists who were in the driver's seat during the writing of the Medicare Prescription Drug, Improvement, and Modernization Act of 2003, the prescription drug portion of which is now infamous as Medicare Plan D. Under the voluntary medication benefit plan, Medicare gives money to insurers through complex subsidies. The insurers then deal directly with seniors and pharmacies. In other words, insurance companies were made the middlemen.

Giving dozens of insurance companies a piece of the action created huge, needless administrative expenses and introduced profit margins absent from the existing Medicare program, further escalating the cost to seniors. Even worse, the fragmented insurance market gives companies little purchasing power to negotiate with pharmaceutical companies for lower drug prices. Most indecent of all, the bill expressly forbids Medicare from using *its* purchasing power to negotiate lower drug prices.

The end result is premiums and copayments that many seniors can't afford and a menu of plans so convoluted it's difficult to understand.

The bill was so awful that the House Republican leadership even had trouble selling it to members of their own party. They literally had to work overtime to pass it.

Votes in the House of Representatives are supposed to last 15 minutes, which is more than enough time for members to get to the floor to vote from wherever they are.

This vote came up at 3 a.m. on a Saturday, at the end of a brutal legislative session. After 15 minutes of voting, which included my emphatic "nay," the bill lacked the 218 votes needed for passage. Instead of declaring the bill defeated, as they should have, the Republican leadership extended the vote. It was like tacking an extra quarter onto the end of a basketball game because you don't like the score at the buzzer.

After 30 minutes, they still didn't have enough votes.

Nor did they after 45 minutes.

On the House floor, Republican "whips," members whose job it is to drum up votes, were putting the hard sell on fellow Republicans who had voted against the bill. Twisting arms and doling out pork were two of former House Majority Leader Tom Delay's fortes.

As the hours went by, I started to wonder whether the leadership was using sleep deprivation to cloud the judgment of colleagues who refused to vote for such demonstrably awful legislation.

Finally, the gavel fell. After three hours—one of the longest votes in the history of the House—the Republican leadership had whipped up 220 votes—two more than the 218 required for passage.

It wasn't a long night just for me. Many constituents, who clearly understood the stakes for their own lives, told me they had stayed up to watch the delayed vote on C-SPAN. It came to be regarded as an infamous spectacle that affirmed long-held stereotypes about the things politicians do in the middle of the night when they hope no one is watching.

- Insurance companies contributed $31,265,381 to campaigns in the 2006 election cycle, including $20,032,365 to Republicans and $10,763,015 to Democrats.[26]

- According to a study that my office conducted with that of Congressman Anthony Weiner (D-NY), the five most popular prescription drugs cost almost twice as much in New York City as they do in France and about one and a half times more than they do in Canada.[27]

- Another study by my office identified one way to cut prescription drug prices: grow two more legs and a tail! In New York, prescriptions purchased for animals—the same drugs at the same dosages—cost less than half as much as those purchased for humans. (For example, uninsured New York seniors paid $109 a month on average for the arthritis drug Lodine; it was available for dogs at $38.)[28]

UNIVERSAL HEALTH CARE

It Can Be Done

With 47 million Americans uninsured and a larger number underinsured, it is abundantly clear that we need to do a better job of providing access to health care. There are many plans on the table: Expand SCHIP to cover adults; allow more people to buy into Medicare; allow people to buy into the federal health-care plans to give them the same choices enjoyed by members of Congress, their staffs, and other federal employees; and offer a single-payer plan, among others.

Unfortunately, while there are many plans, we haven't reached a consensus, and that will take leadership from the White House. Instead of giving us leadership, President Bush has vetoed an expansion of SCHIP and downplayed the need to address the lack of health care. No wonder the number of uninsured has risen so steeply on his watch.

Even some **economists** *can't understand the new Medicare prescription drug benefit. When Plan D first began, my friend Peter, an economist, explored signing up his 81-year-old mother instead of having her prescriptions covered under his own health insurance policy. He told me he spent a week trying to navigate the new system to identify which plan would be best for his mother.*

He ultimately reached the conclusion that his mother might have saved $200 per year out of the few thousand dollars she would spend under Plan D, but that she would have been locked into the plan even if prices increased substantially. The possible savings weren't worth the risk, nor was dealing with the new, confusing system worth the aggravation.

Peter threw up his hands and let the deadline for signing up pass. Many seniors were equally confused and concerned. Unlike Peter's mom, however, most of them didn't have a backup policy to cover their costs.

While the federal government has failed to create an affordable, universal health-care system, one state is making a bold attempt. Massachusetts passed a law in 2006 requiring its 600,000 uninsured residents to purchase health insurance. It's based on laws requiring drivers to carry car insurance. Residents who cannot afford the premiums but are not on Medicaid can receive state assistance to pay for coverage. Anyone who doesn't purchase health insurance may lose their state income tax exemption. Employers must provide health insurance to their workers or pay a fine.[29]

To be sure, implementation has proved challenging. By the end of 2007, only half of previously uninsured residents had enrolled. Sixty thousand people have received waivers from the coverage mandate due to financial hardship. The cost of subsidizing coverage for those who couldn't afford it came in $400 million higher than expected.

But no one said that universal health care would come easy or cheap. And the bottom line is that 300,000 more Massachusetts residents have been newly insured.[30] That's a huge step in the right direction.

But we need to go to work at the national level. I was pleased that all major Democratic presidential candidates proposed universal health care plans.

The one I like best is Senator Hillary Rodham Clinton's.

Senator Clinton's new plan offers the guarantee of health insurance for every American while sharing the costs among all stakeholders, expanding the choices that are available, and building on what works in the current system.

If you like the insurance you have, you keep it. If you don't have coverage or the coverage you have is inadequate, you can choose from dozens of the same plans that are offered to members of Congress, like me, or a Medicare-style public plan. The plan requires all Americans to buy health insurance, if they don't already have it, and offers tax credits to make coverage affordable for all.

Generous tax credits are offered to small businesses to help them afford coverage for their employees, making it easier for them to create jobs with health coverage. Large employers are required to provide coverage and could choose to offer their employees the wide array of plans offered through the health choices menu.

Insurers are required to cover anyone who applies and pays the premiums, regardless of preexisting medical conditions. The reward for taking this on is a bigger risk pool that draws in healthier individuals and tens of millions of additional customers.

Reining in the growth of health-care costs will not be easy, but this plan makes it a priority by promoting health information technology, low-cost generic drugs, and preventive care, while promoting a high-quality system that returns the patient-doctor relationship to the center of the health care equation.

I'm also a longtime cosponsor of a single-payer health-care bill, HR676, sponsored by Congressman John Conyers (D-MI). (*Single-payer* means that the government pays doctors, who are typically in private practice, for care they provide to individuals.)

A well-designed single-payer plan has several potential advantages over the status quo.

1. Most important, everyone gets health insurance. Patients like Linda (see page 92) don't have to postpone early-detection tests because they can't afford them, and earlier treatment is less expensive and avoids risky delays. Patients can choose any doctor they want rather than having to go to the ones included under their private insurance plan or, if they're not covered, to the emergency room.

2. A single-payer plan can also cut costs dramatically. When it comes to health care, the benefits of free-market economics are rivaled by another economic principle: economies of scale. In many industries, the greater the number of identical transactions that are processed, the lower the cost of each transaction. The 1,500 insurance companies in America each process a tiny number of transactions compared to Medicare, our "single-payer" system for seniors. Medicare's administrative costs are typically estimated at 3 to 5 percent of its costs. It benefits from economies of scale and eliminates the expenses of marketing, underwriting, and profit making. The administrative costs for single-payer health-care systems around the world are only slightly higher than Medicare's.

3. Government agencies running single-payer systems save additional money by leveraging bargaining power in transactions with pharmaceutical companies. The Department of Veterans Affairs (which is both a single-payer insurer and a direct employer of doctors) negotiates medication prices with the drug companies. It is able to purchase drugs at as much as a 40 percent discount! The Democratic Congress introduced legislation in 2007 to give Medicare negotiating power, but by October 2007, it had yet to pass the Senate.

4. A single-payer system also eliminates the need for businesses to provide health insurance. For General Motors, the world's largest automobile manufacturer, this could mean a savings of as much as $1,500 per car. Lowering the costs of production would help American companies compete against foreign rivals.

Critics of a single-payer system attack it as "socialized medicine." It isn't. Socialized medicine is when the government actually employs physicians on its own payroll. That's how it's done in Great Britain and other countries. A single-payer system doesn't *employ* doctors, it *reimburses* them out of a single fund—like Medicare.

Critics also claim that a single-payer system would lead to "rationing." I haven't heard many complaints about rationing in Medicare. But health care in America already is rationed by the ability to pay for it. More than a hundred million Americans who are uninsured or underinsured are subject to rationing or the severe financial distress of receiving essential health care they can't afford.

But any single-payer proposal would probably face insurmountable political opposition in the current political climate. Facing extinction, insurance companies would unite against it. People who like the private insurance they have might favor the status quo. And a single-payer system would require much higher taxes.

If other universal health-care plans at the federal or state level fail, a single-payer solution might become more politically viable in the future. But if you support it, don't wait: Tell your representatives today.

We don't even have universal coverage for injured 9/11 first responders and others affected by the poisonous mix of toxins released at Ground Zero. Heroes and heroines rushed into burning buildings and worked on the toxic pile for months. Additionally, some residents, office workers, and schoolchildren were present on 9/11 or encouraged to return to the area by the Environmental Protection Agency that rushed to proclaim the air "safe."

Studies have confirmed that the 70,000 people exposed to the Ground Zero toxins are more likely to develop a variety of ailments—lower fertility rates, respiratory and lung disorders, and mental health problems—and there have been several deaths. Since most people have health insurance coverage through their jobs, when they become too sick to work, they lose their health insurance.

I've been working with the New York congressional delegation to get the affected people the coverage they need. In September 2007, along with Reps. Jerrold Nadler (D-NY) and Vito Fossella (R-NY), I introduced H.R. 3543, the James Zadroga 9/11 Health Compensation Act, which would give those exposed to toxins the right to ask to be medically monitored and guaranteed the right to treatment for exposure-related ailments.

Take-Action Guide

Health Care That's Always There

Our health-care system is an outrage, an international embarrassment, and a human tragedy. Comprehensive health-care reform is *the* social justice issue of our time and the most important women's issue that isn't seen as a women's issue. If every other industrialized country can provide universal health care for about half the cost of our private system and provide better results, the greatest country in the world can and must do the same.

Lots of groups and individuals are working creatively to find new ways to get health care right at the state and local levels and to help the uninsured in their own communities. They're pushing the federal government harder than ever to provide the American people with health care that's always there. If you add your voice to the growing outcry, before long, Washington will have to offer answers instead of the usual excuses.

Because women use the health-care system more, make less money, and are less likely to have health insurance through their jobs, women and their children have the most at stake in health-care reform. I'm convinced that if women don't spearhead broad-based initiatives to forge a system instilled with noble motives and human values, no one is going to do it for us. The cause is nothing less than life itself.

1. Help reform the health-care system so that all Americans have access to affordable, high-quality care.

• **Study the issues and stay informed.** I'm proud that Democratic presidential candidates have come forth with universal health-care plans, and I'm supporting Senator Clinton's plan, which you can learn more about at www.hillaryclinton.com. Go to www.health08.org for news and video coverage from the campaign trail, analysis of health policy issues, and regular public opinion surveys. At www.kff.org or www.kaisernetwork.org, you can also stay up to date on the status of the Massachusetts and California plans and other state and local efforts. Sign up for their Daily Reports—e-mail newsletters that summarize the top news stories on select topics and provide links to the original sources.

• **Get involved by supporting organizations that are actively working for change.** If you're a single-payer advocate, Physicians for a National Health Program is a national organization of 14,000 physicians who support single-payer national health insurance. Their Web site, www.phnp.org, has a section that gives advice on how to help their cause, such as a template showing how to write your own op-ed article. A similar organization, Healthcare-Now!, is a citizens' action group advocating for a single-payer system. They support a bill that I've signed onto, HR676, that would provide single-payer national health insurance for all. Their Web site, www. healthcare-now.org, suggests many ways you can get involved at the grassroots level, including attending or organizing a Healthcare-Now! Truth Hearing to increase awareness about the issue in local communities all over the country.

• **Fight for lower prescription drug costs to allow access to affordable drugs.** Because it is one of the areas in health care that affects Americans most directly, it is essential that we work to lower drug costs. AARP's campaign to lower drug prices, called the Prescription Drug Affordability Campaign, advocates for passage of legislation sponsored by representatives Byron Dorgan (D-ND) and

Olympia Snowe (R-ME) that would allow for the safe and legal importation of prescription drugs from Canada and other approved countries. Go to their legislative action center at www.aarp.org to send an e-mail to your representative in support of the Dorgan–Snowe bill, or call 800-869-3150. They also have an *Rx Watchdog Report* that reports on what the drug industry is doing or not doing to lower drug prices.

2. Help support high-quality women's health and preventive health initiatives to improve our overall health and dramatically decrease treatment costs.

• **Increase access to important health screening.** Early screening has reduced the incidence of certain common and deadly cancers. I am currently working on initiatives that would add coverage for osteoporosis and prostate, breast, and colorectal cancer screening to standard insurance policies. Visit my Web site, http://maloney.house. gov, to learn more.

• **Follow legislation that affects women's health care and write to your representatives to press for their support on these issues.** The National Partnership for Women and Families (www. nationalpartnership.org) provides comprehensive information on women's work, family, and health issues and on pending legislation on Medicare, health insurance, women's medical research, and much more. The Association of Women's Health, Obstetric and Neonatal Nurses Web site has an excellent Legislative Action Center at http:// capwiz.com/awhonn, where you can contact elected officials about pending bills and thank them for their support on past bills. The National Women's Law Center, www.nwlc.org, also has a great section devoted to women's health issues, including federal and state legislation related to Medicaid, Medicare, contraception, health insurance, reproductive rights, and abortion. The National Women's Health Network provides the public with scientifically accurate and complete information about legislative health debates. Visit their Web site at www.nwhn.org.

• **Be your own best health advocate.** Preventing disease by getting regular checkups, getting health screenings at the appropriate times, seeking out high-quality medical care, and being informed about health issues can help ensure your own good health and set a great example for the women around you. And when you are confronted with any medical issues, do your homework so you can make informed decisions about your care. Two great government organizations have consumer-friendly Web sites that provide high-quality information on health issues: The National Institutes of Health (www.nih.gov) and the Centers for Disease Control and Prevention (www.cdc.gov). Consumer Web sites that I find very helpful for information on health, and women's health specifically, include www.webmd.com and www.ivillage.com.

• **Start health education early by teaching our young and teenaged girls about issues that affect them.** Young and teen girls are especially vulnerable to negative messages about health and body image. Help foster positive attitudes early by providing great information and support. The US Department of Health and Human Services sponsors a national education campaign that encourages girls to adopt healthy attitudes and live healthy lives. Visit their Web site, www.girlpower.gov. Take on the tyranny of negative body image! Girls Inc. has a program that helps girls decode and discard unwanted media messages; for more information, go to http://girlsinc.org/ic/page.php?id=1.2.3. At www.mindonthemedia.org/whatyoucando.htm, Mind on the Media has a Take Action section that outlines the standards for ethical advertising and best practices for media depictions of women and girls. They also offer a free Turn Beauty Inside Out Action Kit that promotes a concept of beauty for girls based on "who they are, not how they look." At Dove's Campaign for Real Beauty site, www.campaignforrealbeauty.com, you can download a Mother/Daughter workbook or special workshop guide for a local program. Dove also offers body image exercises and other self-esteem exercises for girls and women, including ideas about things we can do to help one another.

3. Find a way to help the uninsured or underinsured in your own neighborhood.

• **Get involved with charities or foundations that are working to cover the uninsured.** It's estimated that five million children who are currently eligible for state-funded health insurance are not signed up! Visit www.covertheuninsured.org to find out how you can help a campaign that enrolls eligible children in Medicaid and State Children's Health Insurance Programs. You can help plan an event in your neighborhood. Or, learn more about what groups like the Robert Wood Johnson Foundation are doing to cover the uninsured. They sponsor an annual Covering Kids and Families back-to-school campaign that you can get involved with. Visit their Web site at http://coveringkidsandfamilies.org/about/bts to find out how to write letters to your local paper, hand out fliers to parents, plan events, reach out to your local media, get your company involved, and more.

• **Contact your local hospitals to find out how you can help.** Many local hospitals have programs that provide low-cost or free care to people who can't afford it. Reach out to them and offer your time, money, or both to help families in your own neighborhood.

5

FREEDOM FROM FEAR
OF VIOLENCE

"[T]he violence we experience in our own homes is not a personal family matter, it's a public and political problem. It's a way that women are kept in line, kept in our places."

—PATRICIA IRELAND

A soft-spoken homemaker from Williamsburg, Virginia, Debbie Smith is the ultimate symbol of how rape can happen anywhere, anytime, to anyone, no matter how safe you think you are.

On March 3, 1989, in the middle of the day, a man wearing a ski mask, wielding a baseball bat, and claiming he had a knife and a gun entered Debbie Smith's kitchen in bucolic Williamsburg.

Debbie's husband, a police lieutenant, was napping upstairs. Debbie decided not to scream. She was afraid that her husband would run downstairs and get shot. In that split second, Debbie resolved to die without endangering his life, too.

Instead of killing her, Debbie's attacker dragged her into the woods.

He blindfolded her and raped her multiple times. Then he let her go, but not before threatening to return and kill her if she told anyone.

Debbie ran back to her house and woke her husband. All she could say was, "He got me, Rob. He got me."

Immediately relying on his law enforcement expertise, her husband urged Debbie not to shower, for fear of eliminating evidence. Instead, they went to the hospital. Once there, Debbie reported, a doctor "plucked, probed, combed, and swabbed" to collect evidence for the rape kit—DNA samples that are stored for future use. "I felt violated all over again," she said.

In the ensuing weeks and months, Debbie was besieged with recurring nightmares and an all-consuming fear.

"Some people would say, 'At least you're alive,'" she told me. "But to me, that wasn't a consolation. I cursed my attacker for leaving me alive to live with this pain." For a time, Debbie pondered suicide, if she could only make it look like an accident. She said she felt as if she was "detached from everything—a shell, going through the motions."

Though Debbie put on a brave face, her family suffered, too. "Mom did all the things that a mom does," her daughter said years later, "but she wasn't really there."

Finally, in July 1995—more than six years after the horrible attack—Debbie's attacker was identified.

The evidence collected for the rape kit at the hospital—an experience so excruciating at the time—proved to be Debbie's salvation. When the kit was processed some months after the incident, the attacker's DNA was found and entered into a state database.

In 1989, Virginia enacted a law that required all convicted felons to give DNA samples.

Norman Jimmerson, a prisoner who had gone to jail a mere six months after the attack on Debbie, was one of those felons. The sample he gave matched the DNA found with Debbie's rape kit.

That was it; Jimmerson was guilty.

For Debbie, the news changed everything. "For the first time, I took a deliberate breath. I felt I'd been suffocated. Now I wanted that air to fill up my lungs. It felt like freedom, like I had just been let out of prison. I felt like a real human being again."

But when it came time to seek justice, the news was not nearly so good. The local prosecutor told Debbie that despite the DNA evidence, a rape charge would be too expensive and time-consuming to pursue. He wanted to file lesser charges, including abduction and assault.

To Debbie's relief, this prosecutor was replaced before the case came to trial. His replacement was not concerned about the time or the cost; he was determined to prosecute Jimmerson for *all* the crimes he had committed.

Jimmerson eventually received two consecutive life sentences plus 25 years, with no chance for parole.

After the conviction, instead of putting the whole tragic episode behind her, Debbie did the hardest thing of all: She went public with her story. She wanted people to know that rape can happen to anyone, even to the wife of a cop in her own home in broad daylight in one of the safest cities in the country. As she said, it's not just "[women] who are dressed provocatively, have had a few drinks, or made an unwise choice [who are vulnerable]." Debbie wanted it to be clear that rape is not a woman's fault. It is random, so everyone must be vigilant.

- Someone is sexually assaulted every 2½ minutes in America.[1]
- Nine out of 10 sexual assaults are against women.[2]
- One-third of women who have been raped have considered suicide.[3]
- Rape victims are:
    - three times more likely than nonvictims to experience major depressive episodes[4]

- four times more likely to contemplate suicide
- more than four times more likely to develop later drug and alcohol problems[5]

THE SILVER BULLET IS SPELLED D-N-A

Part of my district covers the East Side of Manhattan, one of the safest neighborhoods in New York. But beginning in the 1990s, it was roamed by a sexual predator known in the tabloids as the East Side Rapist. He had terrorized more than a dozen women[6] by 2001, usually raping or sexually assaulting them in the foyers of walk-up apartment buildings late at night.

Ironically, even as the East Side Rapist attacked more and more women, the number of attacks for which he could be prosecuted was at risk of diminishing. The longer the East Side Rapist walked free, the likelier it was that his past attacks would "expire" under the statute of limitations. This is a major obstacle in the prosecution of sexual assault, domestic violence, and child abuse cases around the country. Because of the nature of the crimes—and the reluctance of many victims to come forward—perpetrators often are not captured for years.

It's a phenomenon I've seen time and again. A college intern in my New York City Council office in the mid-1980s told me she had been sexually abused by her mother's boyfriend when she was a young girl. Reflecting on it as a college student, she was furious and wanted to do something about it.

It was heartbreaking to tell her that the statute of limitations had expired, so legally, she didn't have a leg to stand on.

In 2000, while the East Side Rapist was still at large, the Manhattan District Attorney's office came up with an ingenious solution. Adopting an idea that was first used in Milwaukee in 1999, the DA ignored the fact that the East Side Rapist hadn't yet been caught and instead indicted his DNA. Instead of charging him by name, the crime was assigned to something much more concise—his DNA signature. This tactic circumvented statute of limitations provisions; if and when the East Side Rapist was captured, he could be prosecuted for *all* the crimes he had committed.

The case of the East Side Rapist prompted me to look at DNA evidence laws at the federal level. I came across an appalling statistic: Almost 200,000 rape kits were sitting unprocessed in law-enforcement facilities around the country.[7] Many state and local police forces had neither sufficient funding nor the trained personnel necessary to run DNA evidence against databases of criminals' DNA. All the evidence we needed to solve and prevent rape crimes by the tens of thousands was in our hands, but justice wasn't in our budget.

So I organized a hearing of the House Committee on Oversight and Government Reform in June 2001 to look at the issue. But when we reached out to numerous sexual assault victims to ask them to testify, everyone turned us down.

Everyone except Debbie Smith.

"My family and I were not the only victims that day," Debbie said before the committee, her voice cracking slightly. "Every person that touched my life or my family's life was to feel the effect of this crime. They too felt invaded and vulnerable. I could see the pain in their eyes because I was a constant reminder that rape can happen to anyone anywhere."

It takes a lot to make a member of Congress cry, but tears welled up in more than a few eyes.

After the hearings, I authored a bill to authorize grants to reduce the national backlog of unprocessed DNA evidence from sexual assault cases and to train medical examiners in the proper collection and processing of DNA evidence. I was proud to name it the Debbie Smith Act.

The bill should have sailed through Congress. But in Washington, the wheels of change turn slowly. The Debbie Smith Act did not even make it to a vote before the session ended.

So, as the next session of Congress began, I knew I needed one thing to turn the Debbie Smith Act into law: a Republican, as Republicans controlled Congress.

I reintroduced the bill with a co-lead sponsor, conservative Republican Mark Green of Wisconsin, who was a member of the House Judiciary Committee. For the Debbie Smith Act, the road to success would pass through the House and Senate Judiciary Committees. Mark introduced the act and put his heart and soul into passing it.

Senator Maria Cantwell (D-WA), who had initially introduced the Debbie Smith Act in the Senate, reintroduced it along with Senators Arlen Specter (R-PA) and Joseph Biden (D-DE), both important members of the Senate Judiciary Committee. I was pleased that all the new cosponsors had joined the bill, because of both their characters as individuals and their gender. Because women make up less than 15 percent of Congress, nothing can pass both houses unless many men—more than 200—decide that it should.

But getting the right sponsors is only one hurdle in a long process. When an issue doesn't have big corporations and high-priced lobbyists behind it, regular people have to get involved.

We kept up a steady drumbeat at press conferences, forums, and hearings to generate momentum and spread the word about the Debbie Smith Act. Lifetime Television and the Rape, Abuse, and Incest National Network (RAINN) played major roles in garnering the support of grassroots organizations nationwide, whose members prevailed upon their legislators to support the bill.

During the campaign to pass the Debbie Smith Act, I was amazed by the vast number of women who had their own accounts of unsolved rape. In some cases, the news media picked up their stories. The news story that generated the most momentum was a groundbreaking and unorthodox investigation by ABC's 20/20 that aired in 2002. The program provided funding for the city of Baltimore to carry out DNA analysis on 25 open violent crime cases and check the results against state and federal databases of felons' DNA. The city matched the funding, allowing 50 rape or murder cases to be checked.

Out of 39 cases in which usable genetic material was found, four culprits were identified and charged with sexual assault, and one man was exonerated.

This underscored the vast potential of genetic evidence for solving crimes, including rape.

Even Attorney General John Ashcroft announced a separate DNA initiative.

It felt like we were doing everything right in building a consensus within and beyond the Beltway. But then, as so often happens in Congress, the Debbie Smith Act was rolled up into a much larger and more controversial bill, the Justice for All Act of 2004. And, because of a provocative death penalty provision, a single senator was holding up the Justice for All Act.

There was only one person who could change his mind: Debbie Smith.

During the campaign, Debbie had sent handwritten notes to all 535 members of the House and Senate and had met with key members, including this senator. During their meeting, he had promised Debbie that he would support our bill. So Debbie picked up the phone and called the senator. Firmly but politely, she reminded him of his promise.

The senator made good on his promise, and the bill gained final passage. President Bush signed the Justice for All Act on October 30, 2004, and the Debbie Smith Act became the law of the land.

Scott Berkowitz, president and founder of RAINN, has called the Debbie Smith Act the most important antirape legislation ever passed and has projected that it will lead to solving as many as 50,000 open rape cases, taking thousands of rapists off the streets and preventing countless future rapes.

Today, Debbie has found improbable and selfless salvation in the dark events of 1989. "I've had a lot of people say, 'I'm so sorry this happened to you,'" she told me. "But I'm not anymore.... I would have missed out on helping more people in my life than I'll ever meet. What else is life about?"

Debbie's story, and that of the fight to pass the legislation, was made into a movie by Lifetime Television, *A Life Interrupted: The Debbie Smith Act,* with actress Lynn Adams portraying me. Before filming commenced I met with Meryl Streep and made the long-shot request that she play my character. She responded with typical aplomb: "Well, why don't you just play yourself?"

• Through 2004, almost 200,000 rape kits nationwide were unprocessed. Every one of those rape kits represented a life turned upside down and a rapist on the loose.

• In New York, more than 50 percent of felons and 94 percent of those convicted of misdemeanors are still excluded from DNA sampling.[8]

FREEDOM FROM FEAR OF VIOLENCE

BLAMING THE VICTIM

"Are you a virgin?"

It wasn't really a question. It was more of an accusation—the opening salvo of a defense attorney's cross-examination. And it was pretty standard for 1975. That was the year I picked up the *New York Times* and read about a rape case involving a woman who reminded me a lot of myself and very easily could have been me.

I had just moved to New York City and taken a small apartment. Today, New York is one of the safest large cities in America.[9] But at that time, the city was on the verge of bankruptcy and had a more sinister feel. Family and friends warned me to be careful. They saw me as a naïve Southern girl in the big city, and maybe they were right. I shrugged off their concerns—until I read about Kathleen Ham.

An assistant at a publishing firm, she was the same age as I was: 26. She lived in an apartment just like mine in a neighborhood that was just as safe. She was sleeping peacefully in her apartment when an intruder climbed through her window and ruined her life.

It was dark, and he threw a sheet over her head so she couldn't identify him.

During the attack, Kathleen screamed loudly. The cops came right away, chased the intruder from the building, and arrested him across the street. His name was Fletcher Anderson Worrell. (Known by several aliases, he was called Clarence Williams at the time.)

With two cops as witnesses, the prosecution thought they had an open-and-shut case—until the defense asked Kathleen if she was a virgin.

"It was downhill from there," Kathleen told me last year. She found herself on what she now calls "the slut seat." "They tried to make me out to be a hooker. They said I was having a tussle with my pimp. Then they

124

said it didn't happen, that I was making it up, that I was a liar. Then it was 'You wanted it anyway.' It was ridiculous.... The law was there to protect men against women who 'cried rape' or were 'vindictive bitches.'"

The defense grilled Kathleen for a day and a half, accusing her of being a racist and questioning whether a rape really took place.

Doctors from the emergency room testified for the defense, reinforcing the hospital's official report that had also cast doubt on her rape, saying she appeared too calm.[10] "They ignored knife marks on my head and face," says Kathleen. It all added up to a hung jury. Worrell walked.

Kathleen lost her self-confidence. She experienced terrible insomnia. She tried to date again, but without success. "The trust issues were just too enormous," she told me. "Never married, has cats—that's me."

The trauma of the injustice she experienced in court was no small part of what haunted Kathleen. She got a law degree and tried to practice but had lost her faith in the legal system. Her once-promising career was reduced to working temp jobs here and there.

"It affected my life tremendously. If you ever had any feeling that there is right or wrong in this world, or a sense of justice, or a sense of fairness, [the trial] just knocked it out. I became extraordinarily bitter and cynical," she told me.

The entire experience was so traumatic that she decided to spare her parents the pain of knowing about it. Although hundreds of thousands of people read about her case in East Coast newspapers, Kathleen's parents, who lived in California, went to their graves never knowing their daughter had been raped.

Thirty years later, things had changed a little, but not nearly enough.

I met Stacey and Tom Branchini at a stop-violence-against-women event. We spent just about the whole night talking.

A few years earlier, Stacey and Tom's daughter Alexa, a freshman at Boston University, had been repeatedly raped by a man hiding in a shower stall in her dorm's women's bathroom. The suspect, Abdelmajid Akouk, was caught by police 10 minutes after fleeing the dorm.

Akouk's fingerprints were found in the bathroom, and his semen was found on Alexa's body. On top of that, Akouk had sexually assaulted another student outside the dorm building two hours earlier. The trial should have had a quick conclusion.

But the Boston DA cried poor, telling the family there was no money in his budget to pay for DNA testing. Tom Branchini "went bonkers" and said he would pay for the testing himself. The DA was shamed into coming up with the money.

At the trial, Alexa testified that since the rape, she had seen "all the pain and hurt there is in this world" and that "no amount of tears can wash it away."

The defense pulled out all the stops. They painted Alexa as a rich spoiled brat and a troublemaker making false allegations to avoid being thrown out of school. They concocted a story that Alexa had met Akouk at an MIT party earlier that night. Of course, they couldn't find anyone to testify that he had been there, though at age 33 and with a disfigured eye, he would have stuck out like a sore thumb.

The defense made much of the fact that Alexa and her friends "had been drinking" (Alexa drank two beers over seven hours) and that some of Alexa's friends had urinated in the bushes while waiting in a long line outside the MIT party.

There's more. The defense accused Alexa of breaking into an office so she could sneak Akouk in through a window. They accused the Boston University police officers of planting fingerprints.

The sexual intercourse? Consensual. The swelling in her genitals? The result of pleasure, not trauma. The DNA evidence? Useless, since the nurse was a "zealot on a mission." The defense even pointed to a Bob Marley poster in Alexa's room as proof that she was attracted to black men.

The defense went so far as to list Tom and Stacey as witnesses, which precluded them from being present during Alexa's testimony.

After the defense rested, the jury deliberated for three days. By the third day, Alexa had become so unhinged that her parents had to carry her into the courtroom.

Finally, the jury came back with a guilty verdict. The defense had come frighteningly close to succeeding, but it had failed.

After the trial, Alexa's parents established the It Happened to Alexa Foundation. The foundation offers financial assistance so that victims' families can attend trials. Having a family member present is not just reassuring to the victim, it also results in fewer reduced-sentence plea bargains. The foundation also provides victims and their families with emotional support and advice based on the Branchinis' own painful experience. Alexa counsels victims to ignore what defense attorneys say. As she puts it, "For them, destroying your life is just a job."

When I asked Stacey why only about 1 in 10 rapes ever make it to trial,[11] she answered in a voice that blended outrage and anguish. "They make it so hard for the victim to come forward," she told me. "The victim is scrutinized like no other victim. They find some way to make the victim feel guilty. I got a call from a woman in Washington, D.C. Somebody had given her daughter's friend a date-rape drug in her drink. When she got to the emergency room, the police officer berated her for underage drinking. She got so frustrated and upset that she never got a rape kit done. She was never treated for pregnancy [with emergency contraception] or [tested] for HIV. The girl got so scared, she left. They had no evidence to prosecute. This kind of thing happens all the time."

Two differences distinguish Kathleen and Alexa's cases: DNA

A few days after the first anniversary of the passage of the Debbie Smith Act, I picked up the New York Times *to see Kathleen Ham back on the front page. Her attacker had been apprehended after a gun purchase background check revealed longstanding arrest warrants for two previous sexual assaults. He was identified as her rapist with DNA obtained from the underwear. Based on the new evidence, he was retried. Kathleen put aside her trauma and summoned the courage to testify against her attacker again. This time, the jury got it right, and Worrell was sent away to prison.*[12]

Chills went down my spine as I read the story. Thirty-one years after I had despaired over her verdict, it occurred to me that I had not remained as helpless as I had felt at the time to help the Kathleen Hams in our midst. Even before the Debbie Smith Act became law, the publicity we had generated during three years of working to pass it had inspired DAs all over the country to start processing rape kits. Women, Kathleen included, were gaining closure, reclaiming their lives, and rekindling their spirits.

I finally met Kathleen in 2005, when she was honored by the National Organization for Women. Worrell's conviction had certainly helped her. After "a very rough 30 years," her fear has been tempered. She sleeps better.

But Worrell's DNA match brought more sobering news. It also matched the evidence in the rape kits of at least 21 other women who had been attacked in Maryland, New Jersey, and New York. While the matches surely brought closure for those women as well, they underscored the vast human cost and travesty of justice that resulted from the hung jury at Worrell's first trial.

evidence and Alexa's willingness to tell her parents, which may have been rooted in diminished stigma around rape. Today, fewer people—whether jurors, family members, or even rape victims themselves—are receptive to claims that rape is the victim's fault. The societal sense of male entitlement to sex on demand is eroding, while recognition that rape is violence, not sex, is growing. This shift in cultural perception of rape helps explain why rape and sexual assault have fallen by 69 percent since the early 1990s.[13]

But alas, positive outcomes are still the exception rather than the rule for rape victims—by a landslide.

There are far too many similarities between Kathleen's experience in 1974 and Alexa's in 2001: character assassination and painting the victim as a "slut," the claim that the "sex" was consensual, the use of the race card, the attempt to throw numerous concocted allegations against the wall to see what stuck, limited prosecutorial resources.

"When you compare the number of rape cases reported to the number prosecuted, there is only one conclusion: We're not prosecuting sexual assault. We're doing a terrible job," David Lisak, a University of Massachusetts Boston psychology professor, told me. Lisak frequently works with prosecutors on rape cases. He asserts that training for law enforcement officers and prosecutors is inadequate and that funding for prosecution is "pitiful." When it comes to rape, the sad truth is that too little money is providing too little justice.

And while rape shield laws have made it harder to demonize the victim, they are by no means the silver bullet.

With all of the deterrents in the system—limited resources, cultural norms that create or reinforce guilt, fear of character smearing by the defense, and the shocking violations of privacy—it's no surprise that too often, for far too many women, the cost of pursuing the monsters who attack them is just too high.

- An estimated 60 percent of all sexual assault victims don't report attacks.[14]

- Only about 9 percent of sexual assault cases lead to felony convictions.[15]

- In 15 out of 16 cases, the perpetrator never spends a day behind bars.[16]

REAL MEN

Stacey Branchini and I share another lament: a culture of misogyny and entitlement in male American sports. Often this culture, and the public's emulation of it, leads to violence against women and girls.

Male student-athletes commit one in three sexual assaults on campus and are more than twice as likely to be acquitted as other sexual assault defendants.

"Why in America is it that we have come to worship athletes so much that athletes on campus are getting away with horrendous things? We have a very skewed value system," Stacey said.

No one can speak with more authority on the topic of misogyny in sports than Don McPherson. As a quarterback in the National Football League, he spent years in the belly of the beast.

Today, he is the founder and executive director of the Sports Leadership Institute at Adelphi University. But he still goes back into locker rooms to teach professional and college sports teams—and other men and boys in all-male settings—about gender violence prevention.

I met McPherson when he was a fellow panelist at a Lifetime Television event celebrating the passage of the Debbie Smith Act. At the forum, his explanation of why he works so hard to prevent violence against women and girls was as chilling as it was true: "Because we're the perpetrators."

McPherson was an All-American quarterback at Syracuse University and later played for the NFL's Philadelphia Eagles. At a young age, he found himself in the limelight of larger-than-life stardom. But to his surprise, his stardom made him a locus of sinister behavior. "Just my presence as an athlete validated other men and the culture of misogyny," he told me in an interview. "I noticed how quickly men around me would all of a sudden change and morph into this almost Neanderthal language and attitude because they thought I was a safe place."

It always made him uncomfortable, but McPherson didn't know exactly why until he met Jackson Katz, a Northeastern University professor, who put it in the context of violence against women. "It was about sexism. It was about misogyny. It was about patriarchy and an all-male environment that didn't even take into account women, their perspective, or their rights," McPherson told me.

McPherson points to the classic sports epithet "You throw like a girl." "There are two messages inherent in that statement," he said. "We're telling boys, 'Don't be that.' This is how narrow masculinity gets formed. And we're saying, 'Girls are less than.'"

McPherson hopes to expand the definition of masculinity beyond the narrow confines of classic machismo. His goal goes beyond protecting women; he wants to liberate men. "There are very narrow rules that boys have to follow. You're not supposed to cry. You're not supposed to complain. You're not supposed to show any empathy or emotion, especially for anyone or anything. We don't raise boys to be men; we raise boys not to be women, not to be gay," he insisted. "Emotions are tools that give us the ability to deal with everyday life. We need to expand the emotional toolbox. It's not that we need to add anything. We have to allow ourselves and other men and boys to be who we are. We *all* have empathy. We are *all* caring, loving, nurturing. If men don't allow each other to be those things, it becomes the core of misogyny because you begin to hate things that you are but that you're not allowed to be."

I couldn't agree with him more. I've always viewed as a curse the cultural mandate for boys in particular to be "cool," to repress all of

*A **growing number** of prominent men are joining the fight against would-be perpetrators of sexual assault and domestic violence. As a New Yorker, I'm proud that one of those men is Joe Torre. In 1997, when he was manager of the New York Yankees, he did something more important than any World Series victory (although we can always use another one of those): He revealed that he grew up in an abusive household where his father beat his mother. Torre later started the Safe at Home Foundation to combat domestic violence.*

Perhaps the most important thing that women can do to combat gender violence is to persuade the role models whom boys look up to to discourage it. Founding Fathers, a program of the Family Violence Prevention Fund promoted by hundreds of men, including Don McPherson, redefines Father's Day as a day when men give back to their families and communities by saying "no more" to violence against women and children. The simple act of sending this link might be the most important Father's Day gift you could ever give to the men in your life: www.founding-fathers.org.

their emotions, to act as if they are unfazed by everything, to pretend as if they care about no one and nothing, to seem to have everything under control at age 13. It's an emotional starvation diet that robs boys of the joy and enthusiasm that ought to be the birthrights of youth, and violence against women is its by-product.

McPherson contends that chipping away at narrow masculinity will require a sustained long-term effort in a nation where advertising and pop culture bombard Americans with the objectification of women and the depiction, even the celebration, of men as Neanderthals.

"Watch [the TV commercials during] a football game," he said. "How many times are you going to see women being objectified or men portrayed as absolute morons? It's unbelievable how stupid men are in those ads. And here's the sad reality: Men don't *have* to be more evolved. We live in a male-dominated, patriarchal society. All the sophomoric behavior of beer commercials, truck commercials, hardware—that's all men need to be. Men get constantly bombarded with [pickup truck ads]—'It's Ram Tough,' or 'Like a Rock.' It's all a narrow view of what it means to be a man that plays on the collective consciousness of the culture."

And it goes all the way to the White House. "This country went to war, this country has elected a president based on narrow masculinity," McPherson contended. "'You're either with us or against us' wasn't a challenge to Russia or Italy or France; it was a mandate to the American citizen. 'You're either a real American and you agree with this war, or you are un-American.' That's a part of narrow masculinity."

• While male student-athletes comprise 3.3 percent of the population, they represent 19 percent of sexual assault perpetrators and 35 percent of domestic violence perpetrators.[17]

• According to the same study, while 80 percent of sexual assault defendants in the general population are found guilty, the conviction rate for athletes is *38 percent.*

HOME SCARY HOME:
VIOLENCE BEHIND CLOSED DOORS

When you are a member of Congress, virtual strangers often approach you to share troubling, intimate details about their lives. It used to surprise me, but no more. These people are reaching out because they believe—or at least hope—that government can do something to improve their lives.

One day, a woman I hadn't met more than once or twice came up to me on the street. She was distressed. After introducing herself, she quietly undid a few buttons on her blouse, revealing ghastly black-and-blue marks on her chest.

Her husband, she said. He had been assaulting her for many years.

I was shocked. She was not the first woman to tell me she'd been terrorized in her own home; what surprised me was that her husband was a revered minister at a local church.

Intimate partner domestic violence happens everywhere. It can happen to your friends, neighbors, or relatives. It is perpetrated by people of every occupation and all socioeconomic, religious, and racial backgrounds.

But we almost never see it, because it is almost always hidden.

"Partner violence is difficult to measure because it usually occurs in private and because victims may be reluctant to report it due to threats of further violence, shame, or fear of losing their home or even custody of

Some commentators and groups, most notably one called RADAR, promulgate the idea that intimate partner violence is perpetrated against men as frequently and severely as it is against women. RADAR and others, of course, wave studies to back up their case.

It's certainly true that some women do hit men. But the most credible research, including that by the US Justice Department, shows that women are far more likely to be injured during intimate partner violence than men.[18] The distinction between violence—which is unacceptable—and harm—which can be deadly—is critical. For this reason and others, I consider the Justice Department statistics to be authoritative.

That said, intimate partner violence is every bit as reprehensible when women commit it as it is when men do it, and male victims should have equal access to services. As of now, most domestic violence shelter programs serve only women (though most can give a male victim a referral to another facility in the community or county).

This section focuses on women, but I want to be clear: Both women and men whose partners abuse them need services and support that are better than those available today.

their children," Family Violence Prevention Fund president Esta Soler reports.

Until 1994, the federal government had been largely silent on the subject of battered women. That year, Representative Pat Schroeder (D-CO) and Senator Joseph Biden (D-DE) sponsored the Violence against Women Act (VAWA). VAWA strengthened legal sanctions against stalkers, batterers, and rapists; allowed immigrant women leeway to escape their abusers without fear of deportation; and established a toll-free National Domestic Violence Hotline. VAWA also allocated funding for battered women's shelters, rape prevention education, domestic violence intervention programs, and programs to improve both prosecution of perpetrators and victim services.

The bill met with substantial opposition from grassroots groups on the right. One was the Independent Women's Forum (IWF), a right-wing group on whose advisory board Department of Labor secretary Elaine L. Chao currently sits and which once boasted Lynne Cheney as a member of its board of directors. The IWF declared that VAWA was not helpful to assault victims, gave too much authority to the government, was based on exaggerated claims about domestic violence, and was being used by feminists as part of an ideological war against men.[19]

While many conservatives, including some in the current Bush administration, originally opposed VAWA, their collective mindset has come a long way. They deserve credit for creating more than a dozen Family Justice Centers around the country. These centers offer comprehensive services for battered women. All of the services a battered woman might need—from the police, to an order of protection, to a place to stay, to a therapist, to legal services, to health care—are together under one roof. This approach—providing services for victims of domestic violence in a single facility—is an important part of the future for helping and protecting battered women.

But VAWA passed, and President Clinton signed it into law. It has been resoundingly successful.

Carol Sher, who oversees victims' services programs at Beth Israel Medical Center in my district, has been in the business long enough to remember when psychiatrists diagnosed battered women with "masochistic personality disorder," claiming they "wanted" the abuse. She considers VAWA a vital milestone. "Before [VAWA], there wasn't a penny of aid from the city, state, or federal level," she told me. VAWA has also been an important source of funds for law enforcement, which helps give real teeth to domestic violence laws on the books. In addition, VAWA has been a major psychological boost to victims and their advocates and an important awareness builder. It put batterers on notice that they cannot hide forever.

There is no denying that the last few decades have brought significant progress in the battle against violence against women in this country. In addition to VAWA, every state has passed laws identifying domestic violence as a crime. This reflects an improvement in how domestic violence is viewed in our culture.

We need to remember, though, that we started essentially in the Stone Age. "Thirty years ago, in most states, you couldn't rape your wife. There was no such thing as a crime in that situation," RAINN's Scott Berkowitz told me. Domestic violence was largely treated as a "family matter." Cops would look the other way until, in all too many cases, a woman's corpse was wheeled into the morgue. For battered women, life wasn't all that different from that of the proverbial cavewoman being dragged by the hair by a club-wielding Neanderthal.

Unfortunately, the sad truth is that even with VAWA, state and local antiviolence laws, and charitable programs, we are far from being able to meet the need for enforcement and victims' services across this country.

(continued on page 140)

After her first husband died, Susan, who had 14- and 12-year-old children, married a respected surgeon. He and his three children had just moved to Dallas, Susan's hometown. It seemed like a Brady Bunch tale.

But soon the surgeon began to exhibit traditional controlling behavior—prohibiting Susan from leaving their house and curtailing her relationships with friends and family.

Then the beatings began. He ruptured six discs, fractured her tailbone, inflicted a concussion that confined her to bed for three months, denied her medical attention, and in the process, destroyed her self-esteem.

His mental health faltered and he became suicidal. He would wake Susan up, looming over her with a knife in his hand and a belt wrapped around his neck. "If an abuser is suicidal, rarely do they commit suicide without taking someone with them," Susan told me.

Susan endured this horror for 18 years. Finally, she threw some clothes in a trash bag and fled, narrowly escaping her raging husband. She went into hiding. All of her belongings and mementos were left behind. "He totally ruined my life," she told me. "I lost my children. I lost my home. I lost everything."

She also lost in divorce court.

Susan estimates that fully exiting an abusive relationship—going to the police, obtaining an order of protection, finding a place to stay, connecting with a therapist, accessing legal services, acquiring health care, etc.—requires about 30 different steps. Each step brings terror of discovery and retaliation for seeking safety. No wonder so many women stay in abusive relationships or return to them after trying to leave; bureaucratic exasperation, limited access to funds, and false hope during the "honeymoon" reunion often erode a vulnerable woman's will to stay away.

Susan's story worked out better. As she began to rebuild her life, she decided to help others do the same. She launched Women in Transition (WIT), an organization for widows age 45 and older, divorcees, empty nesters, and others learning to cope as newly independent middle-aged women.

Susan teamed up with a WIT member named Linda, whose 31-year abusive marriage had recently ended. Together, the "Two Women," as they call themselves, resolved to bring a Family Justice Center, a federal facility that offers multiple services to domestic violence survivors, to Dallas.

After four years of navigating a bureaucratic maze, the Two Women launched a nonprofit organization, Women on Watch (WOW), and forged a coalition of law enforcement, legal and social service providers, battered women's shelters, and current and former elected officials, who are collaborating on a Domestic Violence Legal Help Center. The center will provide civil and legal services to those affected by family violence regardless of income. Providing these services to survivors at the first intake session helps them avoid having to retell their story frequently and thus reliving traumatic events. This facilitates a more efficient and effective path through the legal and social service communities.

Launching the project was therapy itself. As Linda told me, "It takes a long time to rebuild your self-esteem, to remodel and resculpt your self-image. Every day you get a new chance. . . . I think this is my way of turning the sad times in my life, the pain, into rainbows."

From Washington, D.C., to Washington State, the problems persist: Women are being turned away from battered women's shelters in appalling numbers. There is a widespread shortage of affordable housing for women who need to move into permanent homes. There are too few interventions for children who have witnessed violence. And there are shortages of job training programs and placement services for victims trying to restart their lives.

Even today, according to Kelly Starr of the Washington State Coalition against Domestic Violence, it is too easy for batterers to feel "I can do this; nothing really happens." Think about all the victims who reach the same conclusion.

One generation of gradual reform has brought us out of the Stone Age, but we are still a long way from doing enough. When it comes to domestic violence, our progress has been exaggerated if not greatly, then all too much.

• In the 10 years after the passage of VAWA, overall intimate partner violence fell by more than half.[20]

• Still, according to the US Justice Department, there were 627,400 nonfatal intimate partner victimizations in 2004.[21]

• Victimizations against women outnumbered those against men by more than three to one.[22]

• A third of the attacks were serious violent crimes—rapes, sexual assaults, robberies, and aggravated assaults.[23]

• Three American women are murdered by their husbands or boyfriends every day.[24]

• Various studies show that anywhere from 24 to 52 percent of domestic abuse victims reported losing their jobs because of the abuse.[25]

• Coast-to-coast shelter shortages continue. (For example, Washington, D.C.'s two confidential shelters, which together have 48 beds, turn away as many 350 families a month[26]; in Washington state, battered women's shelters accommodate about 6,000 battered women and children each year but must turn away 35,000 victims.) In 2006, 26 percent of shelter requests by homeless families were denied due to lack of resources.[27]

Take-Action Guide

Freedom from Fear of Violence

New laws and political victories mean nothing to the millions of women who live in fear of violence, who cover their bruises with their blouses knowing that their exit strategy could cost them their lives, who are forced into sexual slavery unless our system—legal, cultural, and moral—reaches them. We must do more to reach the women who cower in the shadows. Here is how you can help.

1. Fight to end sexual assault and rape.

• **Make sure no one who commits sexual assault escapes justice due to insufficient public funding at any stage of the criminal justice process.** Legislators at every level need to hear from you that violence against women must be a much higher priority, that laws need to be passed and enforced and those who break them prosecuted, and that sufficient funding must be appropriated for enforcing provisions like those in the Debbie Smith Act. To learn more about federal legislation, go to http://maloney.house.gov. For information on state and local legislation, go to www.rainn.org, where you can also sign up for its news alerts.

• **Ensure that DNA technology is used in every sexual assault case** before the statute of limitations expires and that it is handled by trained professionals at the crime scene, in the crime lab, and in the courtroom. In addition to pushing for full funding of DNA provisions in the law, urge your state's legislature and attorney general and your local district attorney to establish John Doe indictments using DNA signatures so that sexual assault cases do not expire under the statute of limitations before perpetrators are caught.

• **Educate yourself and others about how to prevent rape.** The Pennsylvania Coalition against Rape offers strategies for staving off or surviving an attack—with a particular focus on date rape and young people—at www.pcar.org/about_sa/stop.html. The Santa Clara, California, Police Department has a good Web page on sexual assault prevention that focuses on personal security and safeguarding your home to avoid stranger attacks at www.scpd.org/crime/sexual_ assault2.html. V-Day began in 1998 with a production of Eve Ensler's *Vagina Monologues* and is now a global movement that raises money and awareness to end all forms of violence against women; visit www. vday.org. If you're a college student, work with Take Back the Night, a leading organization that fights sexual violence on campus: www.takebackthenight.org.

• **Join with Lifetime Television.** With programming, public service announcements, petitions, and lobbying, Lifetime Television is the leading broadcaster fighting violence against women. Every year in March they sponsor a Stop Violence against Women Week in Washington, where activists descend on Capitol Hill to raise awareness and lobby Congress. Find out how you can work with Lifetime at www.lifetimetv.com/community/olc/violence/index.html.

2. Support victims of sexual assault and rape.

• **Make sure that no sexual assault victim feels ashamed or is afraid to seek medical assistance and report an attack.** This one is straightforward, and it begins at home. Tell your kids that no matter what the circumstances, if they are ever sexually assaulted, they should seek treatment immediately. Assure them that your family will be 100 percent supportive and that they will never be blamed in any way. Tell them that they can receive free help, 24 hours a day, from the National Sexual Assault Hotline at 800-656-HOPE, or online at rainn.org.

• **Provide support and financial assistance so that families of sexual assault victims can be present at legal proceedings.** Support the It Happened to Alexa Foundation (www.ithappenedtoalexa.org), which is the only organization I know of that provides financial assistance directly to rape victims and their families so they can be together at trials and other legal proceedings.

• **Help your local rape crisis center.** Many communities now have rape crisis centers in addition to battered women's shelters. They almost always need volunteers and donations. They can advise you of ways you can help prevent sexual assault in your community, as well as providing resources to survivors. To find your nearest rape crisis center, visit www.rainn.org.

• **Team up with RAINN.** RAINN is America's largest organization fighting sexual assault. It works closely with local communities and participates in grassroots efforts. Its Web site, www.rainn.org, is a great resource for virtually any topic on sexual assault, from how to volunteer to how to survive and recover from an attack.

• **Support Hope Exists after Rape Trauma (H-E-A-R-T).** Debbie Smith and her husband, Rob, have a nonprofit organization, H-E-A-R-T, that helps sexual assault victims regain a sense of safety and security. H-E-A-R-T provides information about security devices, trains first responders how to deal with sexual assault incidents, and works with legislators on DNA laws. See www.h-e-a-r-t.info.

• **Reject character assassination of sexual assault victims in the press or in court.** Call in to radio talk shows and write letters to the editor expressing outrage whenever you see attacks on a survivor's character or reputation in a rape case, especially when press coverage is neutral or negative. Participate in or organize protests. Band together with your local rape crisis center or women's organization to raise awareness about the necessity of having—and *respecting*—rape shield laws. On a national scale, write letters to the editor to demand responsible coverage, emphasizing that it is not the accuser who is on trial. Local National Organization for Women chapters offer great ways to get active; find yours at www.now.org/chapters/states.html. You can learn about the rape shield law in your state at http://new.vawnet.org/ Assoc_Files_VAWnet/RapeShield.pdf.

3. Fight domestic violence.

• **Ensure that strong laws are in place and fully enforced.** Educate yourself about and urge your elected officials to support legislation that provides funding and other assistance to battered women's shelters. Three organizations have good Web sites that will keep you up to date on legislative efforts in Washington and around the nation: the Family Violence Prevention Fund (http://action. endabuse.org/fvpf), the National Coalition against Domestic Violence (www.ncadv.org), and the National Network to End Domestic Violence (www.nnedv.org).

• **Work to change men's and boys' attitudes about domestic violence.** The Family Violence Prevention Fund's Coaching Boys into Men program (http://endabuse.org/cbim) calls on fathers, coaches, teachers, siblings, relatives, and mentors to teach boys that "being a man" isn't limited to being tough and in control and that violence against women and girls is wrong. You can also learn more about Don McPherson's work at the Sports Leadership Institute at Adelphi University at http://sli.adelphi.edu. The institute offers programs that inspire leadership through sports while addressing social issues, including violence prevention.

• **Educate Americans on how to avoid, prevent, recognize, and respond to domestic violence.** Start with your kids. Studies of the teen population find that one in five high school girls is physically or sexually hurt by a dating partner.[28] Two excellent Web sites that empower youth to prevent dating violence and get out of unhealthy relationships are www.seeitandstopit.org and www.teenpcar.org. Break the Cycle (www.breakthecycle.org) offers free legal services to young people who are experiencing violence in their relationships or homes and advises on public policy. The Texas Council on Family Violence, which runs the National Domestic Violence Hotline, also runs the National Teen Dating Abuse Helpline at http://loveisrespect.org or 866-331-9474. Learn from the Family Violence Prevention Fund at www.endabuse.org how to recognize when someone is being abused and how to talk to that person.

• **Help bring needed services to your community.** Help bring a Family Justice Center to your community by educating your federal, state, and local elected officials about them. Learn more about them at www.justicewomen.com. Help "the Two Women" assist even more women. To find out how to support their efforts or how to start a center in your area, e-mail them at womenonwatch@sbcglobal.net.

• **Increase the number of shelter beds so that no one is turned away.** Battered women's shelters need the same types of help as rape crisis centers. Find your local shelter by calling the National Domestic Violence Hotline at 800-799-SAFE or going to www.ndvh.org/help/help_in_area.html.

• **Protect domestic violence victims from being stalked or attacked by their abusers at work.** Check with your human resources manager to find out about company programs to prevent domestic violence attacks in the workplace and support workers who are experiencing domestic violence. The National Coalition against Domestic Violence describes how victims and their co-workers and supervisors and managers can prevent on-the-job incidents and get or offer proper support at www.ncadv.org/protectyourself/WorkplaceGuidelines_ 132.html.

6

THE PRETTY WOMAN MYTH

*"Trafficking in human beings is nothing less than a
modern form of slavery."*

—CONDOLEEZZA RICE

I began to learn about the truly evil world of sexual slavery in 1999, when the human rights organization Equality Now contacted me about Big Apple Oriental Tours, a travel company based in my district. The name sounds innocuous enough, but this was not your typical tour company. Its clients didn't turn to it for its expertise on restaurants or cultural landmarks. Big Apple's clients were interested in just one attraction: women. And they all could have gone by the same euphemistic name: John.

Big Apple was a "sex tourism" business. It arranged tours of seedy nightclubs in Thailand and the Philippines. These nightclubs were thinly veiled brothels, of course. Big Apple even advertised access to virgins. An Associated Press reporter who viewed one of Big Apple's "promotional videos" reported that it contained a clip of a Filipina woman identifying herself as "17 years young."[1]

From the moment I learned about Big Apple, I wanted to put them out of business.

But in 2000, a gap in the law prompted the Queens District Attorney and US Attorney General to decide against pursuing an indictment against the men who ran Big Apple—Norman Barabash and Douglas Allen. Based on the laws at that time, there was insufficient evidence to prove that Big Apple's customers traveled "with intent" to have sex with minors—the threshold for criminal conduct.[2]

Barabash was so bold that he sent me a letter and brazenly posted it on his Web site. Here's an excerpt.

> ... have you now exposed your true political affiliation to be the champion of lesbian extremists ... that believe that marriage is sexual servitude and bondage? A school of thought that says all men are rapists, wife beaters and child molesters? A school of thought that has nothing more positive to say about men than that they are the source of all evil in the world? A school of thought that believes it is more important for women to be domineering rulers of society than to be conscientious mothers and wives? A school of thought that is actively working to change the world to a matriarchal dictatorship run by a few rich nags?

I guess he didn't appreciate my interest in his work.

Despite Barabash's swagger, we—myself, Equality Now, Gloria Steinem, and other committed elected officials—continued to pursue Barabash and Allen. In 2003, New York's then–attorney general Eliot Spitzer won a temporary restraining order, effectively crippling Big Apple's ability to do business. In early 2004, Barabash and Allen were indicted under New York State law—the first criminal action of its kind against a sex tourism company. Though the case was dismissed on technical grounds in 2004, Barabash and Allen were reindicted in 2005.

Charges were dismissed in 2006, underscoring the need for stronger laws. But the process sent a strong message to sex tourism companies across the nation that their actions will be scrutinized and that it might be best to close up shop.

Learning about sex tourism gave me a window onto a broader world that extends into the darkest reaches of the human soul and takes its victims to the outer limits of human suffering—sex trafficking, a legal term that is really just a euphemism for sexual slavery.

More people in the world may be enslaved today than there were in the 19th century (some estimates run as high as 27 million). The largest categories of extant slavery, sex slavery and domestic servitude slavery, overwhelmingly affect women and girls. Sex tourism is a significant driver of sex slavery, the third-largest and fastest-growing source of revenue for organized crime—a vicious criminal industry that President Bush rightly calls "a special evil."[3]

Nuch was working as a maid in Bangkok when a trafficker promising her a lucrative job in a Thai restaurant lured her to Tokyo. The young woman, who had only a fourth-grade education, was told that she would merely have to pay off a small debt for expenses when she got to Tokyo.[4] But once in Japan, she was robbed of her passport, fed birth control pills, and coerced into working as a prostitute at two late-night snack bars. She had to sexually service several often drunk and dirty customers a night. And she was stuck: The more money she made, the more her captors increased her "debt."

Nuch was warned to hide the fact that she came from Thailand, because Japanese men feared Thai women had AIDS. One night, Nuch slipped and told a client where she came from. When her client left, her captors beat her. "If you tell another person you are Thai again, you will have a name, but no body," they threatened. After many months, the police swept in and arrested everyone, including Nuch. She served several months in solitary confinement before Japanese authorities sent her home to Thailand.

Then the worst news came: She tested positive for HIV. It might have surprised her Japanese johns to discover that it was they, not she, who were the real risks.

Since 2000, when I was dismayed to learn how hard it would be to shut down Big Apple Oriental Tours, some improvements have been made on behalf of women like Nuch. Congress passed and President Bush signed laws that help prevent human trafficking overseas by holding countries accountable for making progress in fighting it, support trafficking victims in the United States, and impose severe penalties on traffickers both here and abroad. Today, sex traffickers who exploit children under the age of 14 by using force, fraud, or coercion can be imprisoned for life in the United States. Thanks to a provision in the PROTECT (Prosecutorial Remedies and Other Tools to End the Exploitation of Children Today) Act, a bill I supported when it passed Congress in 2003, any American who has sex with a minor in a foreign country can go to jail *in the United States* for 30 years—billboards greeting visitors in Phnom Penh and Bangkok read "Abuse a child in this country, go to jail in yours."

Provisions of a comprehensive human trafficking bill signed into law in 2005 expanded victim assistance, broadened US courts' jurisdiction to cover additional trafficking offenses committed by Americans abroad, authorized prosecutors to go after traffickers on money laundering and racketeering charges, and began to address the demand side of the equation in the United States, as we had so aggressively done overseas.

When we were working to pass it, Representative Deborah Pryce (R-OH), the highest-ranking woman in the House at the time, recruited me to be the lead Democrat on the demand-side provisions. The End Demand for Sex Trafficking Act, which contained those provisions, was folded into a broader antitrafficking bill that became law. As Deborah said on the House floor, "There is no politics in the sex trade. And when this body is constantly portrayed as bitterly partisan, it is a joy to provide one more example that this is not the case."

The best definition of evil I've ever heard is that it is simply the absence of empathy. The trafficking of girls and women—robbing them of every shred of dignity, which is every human's birthright, strictly to make a profit—is evil in the extreme.

- Of the estimated 27 million people held in slavery around the world today:
    - 80 percent are female
    - as many as 50 percent are minors
- 800,000 people are trafficked across international borders each year.
- 14,500 to 17,500 are trafficked into the United States.[5]

EXPLOITATION BY ANY NAME

I met Angela through Lifetime Television. In testimony before Congress, she helped me understand that sex trafficking is not just a foreign problem.

Angela was 10 years old when her new foster mother's boyfriend began abusing her. Not long after, the boyfriend began forcing Angela and her foster brother to have sex with men for money.

Angela was eventually removed from the foster home. She was placed in a youth center. At age 14, she ran off with an older man who promised her the world. "We had a great plan about us living together, making money together, and becoming rich. I thought this was everything I had always wanted," she testified.

Then he told her that she had to help him make money.

Her boyfriend turned out to be a pimp. Like thousands of other vulnerable girls, Angela had been lured into sexual slavery: an often shortened life full of pain, torture, and degradation. Pimps often use charm and promises to recruit girls into prostitution, creating what has been called love addictions. The girls realize too late that they have to make money for the men, who are essentially slave masters.

The pimp forced Angela to have sex with his friends in a motel room. He then turned her out onto the streets of Chicago with a quota to meet: $500 for a night's work.

She did one trick and returned to the pimp with only $50. He beat her and sent her back out onto the street. She stayed out until she had made her quota—at 10 p.m. the next night. When she returned, he took the money and sent her out again, demanding another quota. When she returned the next morning, he took the money she'd gotten and forced her to sleep in a closet.

Angela was too terrified to try to escape. She felt like she had nowhere to go. The foster care system had let her down one too many times. She resigned herself to her plight.

So 14-year-old Angela walked the streets of Chicago, turning as many as 10 to 15 tricks a night just to avoid being beaten by the pimp.

Fortunately, she was arrested, and her life as a prostitute ended. She was returned to adoptive parents and was given the chance to slowly rebuild her life.

When Angela and I had a meeting and she expanded on her story, I found it so unbearable that I kept interrupting her. When you work in public service and focus on the issue of child welfare—as I had on the New York City Council—and the system fails a child so completely that she attempts suicide and is forced to survive by turning tricks on the street, you feel like a failure, too.

Sitting there, hearing Angela's story, I connected the dots in a way

I never had before. There is a straight line between neglect, child abuse, prostitution, and sex trafficking. Although there had always been streetwalkers in plain view in my district, I had never fully understood the nature of street prostitution. It is sex trafficking by another name.

To many, street prostitutes are luridly fascinating. Motorists strain their necks to gawk at them in their gaudy, skimpy clothing and spike heels. "Hookers" are often depicted in movies as savvy, alluring adults turning tricks of their own free will to pad their wallets.

Angela's story and countless others like it are grim reminders to all of us that the reality is much more sordid. Pimps trick or even kidnap young girls. They constantly threaten violence. They push them to use drugs and alcohol, creating addictions that increase the girls' dependence on them.

Sexual slavery is in our midst—on the street, at strip clubs, in massage parlors, and behind closed doors. We prefer to think of sex trafficking as something that only happens overseas, but sadly, it's in our own backyard too.

So the next time you see a "hooker" on the street, remember that you're not looking at some sort of entertaining sideshow; you are most likely staring tragedy—and a new kind of American slavery—square in the face.

In 2006, with Angela's story ringing in my ears, I spoke at a rally organized by GEMS—Girls Educational and Mentoring Services—which assists New York City girls who have been, or are at risk of being, sexually exploited or abused. Many survivors of prostitution were there. I asked a few about the idea of legalizing prostitution. I've always opposed legalization, and so did they.

We agreed that without the stigma and risk of illegality, demand

It is incumbent upon all of us to raise the public's consciousness and speak out against misleading portrayals of prostitution in popular culture.

Rachel Lloyd, founder and executive director of Girls Educational and Mentoring Services (GEMS), told me that the ultimate feel-good "chick flick," 1990's Pretty Woman, *did tremendous damage to the public's perception of prostitution. But it wasn't just that one movie. Recently,* New York *magazine glamorized ultra-high-end prostitution with a story about an escort service. A beautiful, naked woman draped in a sheet was pictured on the cover. Supposedly, her services cost $2,000 a trick. She said she loved her work and got out of the business after her benevolent boss was arrested.*[6]

The Academy Award for Best Original Song in 2006 went to "It's Hard Out Here for a Pimp," whose abhorrent lyrics are nothing to honor. People host "Pimps and Hos" parties— including one in New York City—where real-life pimps are honored as heroes. There are television shows like MTV's Pimp My Ride, *in which the word "pimp" as a verb has come to mean making something fancy. Even the venerable* New York Times *ran a story on barbecuing called "Pimp My Grill."*

The end result is a widespread perception that prostitution is a "victimless crime" or even a glamorous career choice for beautiful women.

The apathy, and worse, that goes along with that perception is dangerous for women and girls everywhere.

would soar. Then supply would have to come from somewhere. Inevitably, the supply would come, at least partially, from illegal trafficking.

Legalization of prostitution in other countries has borne this out. In Australia, legalization led to a huge increase in illegal prostitution, as organized crime groups stepped up sex trafficking activities.

The women at the GEMS rally and I agreed that law enforcement efforts should focus on the traffickers, not the exploited victims. We're still largely stuck in an era in which courts are convicting slaves of slavery and letting their slave masters walk.

But convicting the pimps and traffickers is complicated.

Norma Hotaling, executive director of an education and outreach group called SAGE (Standing Against Global Exploitation) had been a drug-addicted prostitute for 21 years in San Francisco when she found herself "facing death" if she didn't make radical changes in her life. She turned herself in, got clean, and started giving her time to help her former peers: women on the street who are addicted and dependent on the sex trade, terrorized by pimps, and at the mercy of their johns.

"At that time, the outreach services were basically handing out condoms and bleach [to sterilize needles] to women and girls on the street," she told me.

Neighborhood groups in San Francisco would attack the prostitutes on the streets, throw balloons filled with bleach at them, and call meetings with local police to demand stronger crackdowns on prostitution. Determined to form alliances that would cut down on prostitution without revictimizing prostitutes, Hotaling appealed to her former foes, tapping neighborhood groups and police to develop more constructive approaches.

Federal prosecutions have focused on cases involving trafficking across state and international borders for purposes of enslavement. But Bradley Myles of the Polaris Project, an advocacy organization fighting human trafficking and modern-day slavery, says the word "trafficking" is often misinterpreted. As he told me, "Many people hear the word 'trafficking' and associate it with transportation. But under current law, transportation is not required for a criminal conviction for human trafficking. While an act of human trafficking can include transporting victims, in the criminal justice system, the 'trafficking in persons' federal law is understood more like involuntary servitude and/or the buying or

When she had lunch with the head cop of the unit that had arrested her more than 30 times, she offered to put together an educational curriculum for the men who were soliciting prostitutes. He agreed. The pilot program, attended by 13 men who were sentenced to it, was the first incarnation of "John School."

Hotaling has shaped John School into an enormously successful rehabilitation program that's being duplicated around the country by various groups. At John School, "students" learn what prostitution is really about. Appealing to johns' empathy and decency sometimes enables their better instincts to prevail over their baser ones.

Hotaling played a vital role in shaping the End Demand Act by successfully emphasizing the importance of education and funding for state and local grassroots programs.

Her work is a great reminder that working together, communities, cops, politicians, and victims of the sex trade can abolish the scourge of 21st-century American slavery.

selling of human beings." To most enslaved prostitutes, transportation matters little. Sex slavery, rape, and torture are unbearable whether you are around the corner or around the world from where you began (although being taken across borders to unfamiliar locales, especially foreign countries where an unfamiliar language is spoken, does make escape more difficult).

Federal law requires a higher burden of proof—force, fraud, or coercion—than state and local "pimping" laws. Under the latter, pimps can more easily be prosecuted and imprisoned for promoting prostitution, statutory rape (most pimps have sex with their girls), endangering the welfare of a child, and forced detention. On the other hand, the sentences handed down for breaking local pimping laws are often too lenient. Rachel Lloyd, founder and executive director of GEMS, has seen pimps get 30 years under federal law but as little as two months under local laws for the same infractions.

In recent years, 27 states have passed trafficking laws that generally carry stiffer penalties than traditional pimping laws. That means that 23 states have not.

With the Trafficking Victims Protection Act up for reauthorization, we have a chance to make a revolutionary change in the way trafficking is prosecuted and to create a model for the states by removing barriers that make it virtually impossible to prove a case. As it stands now, to obtain a federal conviction, prosecutors have to prove that a victim was subjected to force, fraud, or coercion. It takes an exceptionally brave victim to stand up in court against the individuals who persecuted her. Over and over, advocates have told stories of traffickers walking free because their victims are too afraid to testify. We need to rectify the imbalance that allows those victimized by sex trafficking to bear the brunt of law enforcement efforts, while their exploiters walk away unpunished.

That's why I am pleased that in December 2007 the US House of Representatives overwhelmingly passed the William Wilberforce Trafficking Victims Protection Reauthorization Act (H.R. 3887), which would allow the Justice Department to prosecute sex traffickers without having to prove force, fraud, or coercion or a victim's status as a minor, while at the same time allowing prosecutors to use such aggravating circumstances as the basis for enhanced penalties. We are awaiting Senate action on the bill.

Unfortunately, a coalition has materialized to oppose passage. Among the leaders of the opposition are career attorneys in the Bush administration's Department of Justice who are waging an all-out effort to eliminate key provisions of the House bill.

We are fighting back with a strong group of supporters. The Coalition Against Trafficking in Women, comprised of more than 100 leaders across the religious, political, and intellectual spectrum, have sent to a letter to Senate leadership calling for passage. As co-chairs of the Anti-Trafficking Coalition, Congresswoman Thelma Drake (R-VA) and I wrote a letter asking for a meeting with the president and, along with Congressman Robert C. Scott (D-VA), we are circulating letters in Congress in support of the bill. We should no more legitimize pimps than those who invaded African villages, kidnapped people, brought them in chains to America, and sold them like cattle to the highest bidder.

The social action–oriented evangelical magazine *Prism* made the strongest case against it I have ever seen by publishing mug shots of women and girls arrested for prostitution (see photos on page 246). The first shot follows their first arrest—they look normal. By the last shot, they are drawn and disheveled, with hollow eyes and bruises. Shorn of all dignity, ravaged by Johns, battered by pimps, they've been reduced to mere husks of human beings. Like Angela's story, their faces haunt me and, like Angela, they inspire my work on sex trafficking.

I'm legislating on the House side for yet another approach to end pimps' reign of terror that Senator Charles Grassley (R-IA) came up with: Provide the IRS with the resources to go after traffickers for tax evasion. This same tactic landed Al Capone in jail when efforts to convict him of other crimes failed.

Unfortunately, laws are just words on a page if law enforcement agencies and officers don't enforce them. Even though the laws are getting better, federal agent Martin Ficke, who oversees US Immigration and Customs Enforcement's New York division, told New York's *Daily News*, "I've been in this business for 30 years—[sex trafficking] is much more prevalent now than it was then."

I guess that protecting powerless girls and women—especially when most people consider them to be criminals themselves—is rarely a high priority for a district attorney or attorney general.

You call this progress?

• Of the 450,000 kids who run away from home each year, one in three are lured into prostitution within 48 hours of leaving home.[7]

• The average age of girls entering prostitution is 12 to 14.[8] According to some advocates, it is even lower.

• In Minnesota, nearly 50 percent of girls and women in prostitution who were surveyed had attempted suicide.[9]

• Eighty-nine percent of prostitutes want to get out of the business.[10]

• In an Oregon study, 80 percent of girls and women in prostitution had been sexually assaulted by their pimps.[11]

• The mortality rate of women and girls in prostitution, adjusted for age and race, is more than 200 times greater than that of the population at large.[12]

Take-Action Guide

The Pretty Woman Myth

1. End the demand for and supply of prostitution in the United States.

• **Decrease the demand for prostitution.** Work with your local community, parent-teacher organizations, churches, and other neighborhood groups to pressure the police into enforcing local laws against pimps and johns. Ask the chief of police whether arrested prostitutes are screened for slavery. Support SAGE (www.sagesf.org) and similar programs that address the demand side of sex trafficking by educating johns in "John School" and using the fees collected to help teens and adults leave conditions of commercial sexual exploitation and prostitution. Spread the word that prostitution is a brutal human tragedy, not an entertaining sideshow or "quality of life" nuisance in their neighborhood, and reach out to help its victims rather than ostracize them.

• **Decrease the supply of prostitutes.** Demand that sex traffickers and pimps be prosecuted as the slave masters and kidnappers they usually are, that drastically stiffer sentences be imposed upon their conviction, and that new ways to criminalize their activities be enacted. Sign up for Polaris Project's policy alerts on federal and state legislation at www.polarisproject.org/index.php?option=com_content&task=view&id=50&Itemid=69.

• **Help "deglamorize" prostitution.** If you hear a song glamorizing "pimps and hos" on the radio, call the station and explain that it offends you and why. If a local theater runs a movie celebrating pimps, write a letter to the manager explaining why you and your friends won't see it. Follow that up with a letter to the editor of your local paper. Ditto if you see a newspaper or magazine story that engages in similar glamorizing. Distribute news stories and spread the word about television reports and films that accurately portray the exploitative nature of prostitution and sex trafficking. Anytime you hear a joke about prostitutes, explain why nobody should be laughing.

• **Urge your legislators to support better and stronger legislation.** This includes my bill that would prosecute pimps and sex traffickers by using the same tax-evasion laws that put powerful members of the mafia behind bars. It also means removing the fraud, force, and coercion standard for convicting sex traffickers so prosecutions of pimps and slave masters can be expanded. Also support the reauthorization of the Trafficking Victims Protection Act of 2000, which includes my End Demand for Sex Trafficking Act. Urge your legislators to reject DOJ's proposed weakening of the bill that deems prostitution "labor or services."

• **Make sure children—starting with yours—are not coerced or tricked into sexual slavery or prostitution.** Make sure they know the dangers and how to keep themselves safe. The National Center for Missing and Exploited Children has posted some good resources that will help you talk to children, as well as safety tips that are of value to both teens and adults, at www.missingkids.com; click on Resources for Parents & Guardians on the left side of the screen. You can also learn if sex offenders live near you at www.familywatchdog.us. Sign up to be notified for free when a registered sex offender moves to within five miles of you.

• **Work with local victims' services providers to have speakers talk to your local schools, community groups, or neighborhood coalitions.** GEMS, which specializes in helping girls, organizes educational programs for youths, and can connect you to groups in some parts of the nation. Check their Web site, www.gems-girls.org, to find out how you can support their other efforts.

2. Fight to eradicate sex trafficking at home and abroad.

• **Support efforts to end overseas trafficking,** including those run by Equality Now (www.equalitynow.org) and the Coalition against Trafficking in Women (CATW; www.catwinternational.org). Equality Now's efforts include fighting mail-order bride companies and US military personnel's patronage of sexually exploited trafficked girls and women. The CATW has an international focus that addresses both the demand and supply sides of commercial sexual exploitation.

• **Urge the president to sign and the Senate to ratify the 1949 UN Convention for the Suppression of the Traffic in Persons and of the Exploitation of the Prostitution of Others.** This UN convention, already signed by more than 70 nations, directly calls on nations to address the demand for sex trafficking victims.

• **Read the US State Department's annual *Trafficking in Persons Report* and refuse to visit countries that are ranked in Tier 3,** the lowest tier, at www.state.gov/g/tip. In your travels abroad, if you find out any information on sex trafficking, report it to that Web site.

• **Seek out civic and church groups that help rescue and heal the survivors of sex trafficking abroad.** When you contact your town or city council or police department to inquire about local laws, also ask whether there are any local groups providing services to victims. ECPAT has established a "New Underground Railroad," an alliance of churches and faith organizations of all beliefs working together to bring an end to child sex trafficking (for more, visit www.ecpatusa. org). Polaris has a grassroots action page that allows you to decide how much time you want to devote to combating sex trafficking, from as little as five minutes to full-time, at www.polarisproject.org.

7

★ ★ ★

A WOMB OF OUR OWN

"No woman can call herself free who does not own and control her body. No woman can call herself free until she can choose consciously whether she will or will not be a mother."

—MARGARET SANGER

One day when I was in high school in the 1960s, I got a call from the mother of one of my classmates. She told me her daughter was pregnant. My friend's mother was calling to ask me to tell my friend that I still respected her.

I instantly knew that my classmate's life had been irreversibly altered. I could only imagine her and her family's anguish. How desperate they must have been to make that phone call, to plead with their daughter's peers not to ostracize her.

But in that day and age in Virginia Beach, I knew why they felt they had to plead. My feeling was borne out by the reaction of my peers. Though I extended my support to the girl, too many of my classmates did not. The blouses my friend wore may as well have been branded with a scarlet letter P for pregnancy.

My friend had had sex in spite of a strong message—from her parents

165

and others—to remain abstinent. She may not have known anything at all about contraception. If she did, she certainly didn't learn it at school. Of course, her pregnancy suggested that whatever she did know, it hadn't been enough.

Back then, the only real option she and her parents had was to make those difficult phone calls. The next time I saw her, I could tell from the shame and sadness on her face that she desperately did not want to give birth at such a young age. But her only other option was to break the law and risk her life with a back-alley abortion—if she could find someone, hopefully a doctor, to do it.

We haven't regressed all the way back to the mid-'60s, but we're getting dangerously close. Of all the issues discussed in this book, reproductive rights have experienced the worst backsliding in recent years. Things today are far worse than they were in the wake of *Roe v. Wade* in 1973. Reproductive health care that allows women to manage their own fertility and saves and improves women's lives is under assault by a well-organized, well-financed, anti-choice movement that extends all the way to the White House. The movement we're fighting flies in the face of reproductive justice at every turn. Its advocates oppose providing kids with comprehensive and medically accurate sex education; vaccinating young women against a potentially life-threatening sexually transmitted infection; preventing unwanted pregnancy and reducing the need for abortion through contraception and emergency contraception; and protecting women's right and access to a safe and legal abortion. Instead, they prefer to try to install a puritanical, utopian fantasy world. In the *real* world, their unflagging pursuit of this fantasy only produces more unwanted pregnancies, abortions, sexually transmitted diseases, infertility, and fatalities.

For too many students, this means that when it comes to learning what they need to know about sex and contraception, the situation now is not much better than it was 40 years ago.

Since shortly after the dawn of the Bush administration, Democratic members of Congress have been able to do little more than try to raise the public's awareness as the executive branch, with rubber-stamp approval from previous Republican majorities in the House and Senate and help from ultra-conservative judges, have rolled back advances that we have protected for a generation.

That's why, in 2005, I felt compelled to conduct a reality check to discover whether the president was with us here in the 21st century. I decided to ask him whether he believes in birth control.

Little did I know that the request would morph into an object lesson in shaming a public official into answering an uncomfortable question and in the value of persistence, whether you're a politician, journalist, or student activist.

It started with a follow-up question at a White House press briefing on May 26, 2005. That day, radio talk show host Les Kinsolving had a testy exchange with former White House press secretary Scott McClellan. It went like this.

KINSOLVING: There are news reports this morning that parents and children who were guests of the president, when they visited Congress, wore stickers with the wording, "I was an embryo." And my question is, since all of us were once embryos, and all of us were once part sperm and egg, is the president also opposed to contraception, which stops this union and kills both sperm and egg?

MCCLELLAN: I think the president has made his views known on these issues, and his views known—

KINSOLVING: You know, but what I asked, is he opposed—he's not opposed to contraception, is he?

MCCLELLAN: Well, and you've made your views known, as well. The president—

KINSOLVING: No, no, but is he opposed to contraception, Scott? Could you just tell us yes or no?

MCCLELLAN: Les, I think that this question is—

KINSOLVING: Well, is he? Does he oppose contraception?

MCCLELLAN: Les, I think the president's views are very clear when it comes to building a culture of life—

KINSOLVING: If they were clear, I wouldn't have asked.

MCCLELLAN:—and if you want to ask those questions, that's fine. I'm just not going to dignify them with a response.

Oh, my, I thought as I reviewed the exchange, *does* this president believe in birth control? So I rounded up 18 members of Congress to cosign a letter asking him. We didn't hear anything, so we sent a second letter on August 1. "Responsible men and women need [you] to stand up in support of their rights to contraception, not to shy away from the issue," we implored.[1]

Weeks and months went by. No word from the president.

On October 25, 2005—the day after we sent a third letter—Kinsolving quizzed McClellan again, noting that 32 members of Congress were now pressing for a response. Again, McClellan evaded. "What the focus has been from this administration is on promoting abstinence programs that ought to be on the same level as the education funding for teen contraception programs," he said, evading the question completely.

Still confused, we wrote a fourth letter seeking clarification.

Mr. President, does this mean that abstinence is the heart of your birth control policy? Mr. McClellan mentioned teens, but what about married women, college women, working women, women in the military, divorced women, mothers who don't want more children? Do you think that promoting abstinence should be their birth control method as well?

If so, then this position is a radical departure from previous administrations, and undermines women's Constitutional right to birth control that has been respected in this country since the landmark 1965 [Supreme Court] case *Griswold v. Connecticut.* ... We are truly worried that for the first time in decades, access to birth control is in doubt. ... Is Scott McClellan's October 25 statement your answer to the question are you for or against birth control, or is your birth control policy abstinence-only? ... Again, Mr President, please set the record straight.

Silence.

Finally, in the wake of a *New York Times Magazine* cover story detailing how extreme-right groups allied with the president were waging a fight against birth control, 42 of my colleagues and I decided to drop the president one more note.[2]

By that time, the president's approval rating had plummeted. McClellan had resigned. The White House's next press secretary, former radio talk show host and Fox News anchor Tony Snow, was more charming and clever than his predecessor, and his relationship with the White House press corps was less adversarial.

So this letter, our fifth, prompted Kinsolving to pose the old question to the new man at the lectern in a more jocular way: "Tony, as the only other talk radio host in this room, I'd like to ask you as a former colleague a brief, one-part question. [Laughter.] Congresswoman Maloney of New York and 43 [*sic*] others in the House have written the president, and this is the fourth [*sic*] time with no response from [him], to ask, Is the president opposed to contraception or not?"

After a little banter, Snow gave an answer that was more artful than McClellan's had been, but no more illuminating: "The president does not share his private correspondence with members of Congress or others, and so I don't have an answer for you, Lester."

And then, on May 25, the Red Sea parted, Red Sox fans professed love for the Yankees, there were free ice skating lessons in hell, and the administration replied—308 days after our first letter—in the affirmative. Replying on the president's behalf, the assistant secretary for health in the Department of Health and Human Services, John O. Agwunobi, wrote, "This Administration supports the availability of safe and effective products and services to assist responsible adults in making decisions about preventing or delaying conception." In other words, *yes.* Or actually, *yes, but.* The letter continued: "Additionally, this Administration strongly supports teaching abstinence to young people as the only 100 percent effective means of preventing pregnancy, HIV, and sexually transmitted infections."

We'll never know why this change occured—whether Snow decided that he didn't want to have to dodge this question again; whether the president's new chief of staff, Joshua Bolton, decided it was time to be more responsive to Congress; or whether silence on birth control would be a political liability for Republicans in the upcoming Congressional election.

Still, it was an answer that my allies and I agreed with wholeheartedly.

But it gave rise to a new question: When would they start to walk the walk?

- Sixty-three percent of teens have sex by 12th grade. More than one-third of kids have sex by 9th grade.[3]

- Seventeen percent of sexually active females and 9 percent of males between ages 15 and 19 reported using no method of contraception the first time they had sex.[4]

- Thirty-one percent of all women become pregnant before age 20. Thirteen percent of sexually active men between the ages of 15 and 19 report fathering a pregnancy.[5]

• Approximately 80 percent of teenage pregnancies are unintended, accounting for one-fifth of all accidental pregnancies in the United States.[6]

ABSTINENCE-ONLY DREAMING

My daughters were lucky that they got comprehensive sex education at school. I was lucky they got it, too. Based on the information they relayed to me, their teachers did a much better job of educating them about sex than I could have, despite my best efforts.

Don't misunderstand me: Most parents, myself emphatically included, want their children to refrain from having sex until, at the very least, they are emotionally and physically mature and involved in a loving, committed, and monogamous relationship.

But the painful truth is that neither fear of sex nor exclusively teaching about abstinence is going to stop millions of kids from having sex. As Tamara Kreinin, former president of the nonprofit Sexuality Information and Education Council of the United States, put it, "The real success of the abstinence-only-until-marriage movement has been the ability of its leaders to shape the debate.... Such programs became palatable to many communities because they provided messages that adults were eager to hear: If we tell our young people not to have sex, they won't."[7]

If that were true, there would be no debate. But the fact is that the more kids know about contraception, the less likely they are to find themselves in the predicament my classmate did in the 1960s or to be faced with a sexually transmitted disease.

Sensible, practical people recognize that education about contraception is not an endorsement of sex but rather a way to govern in a less than ideal world.

It's much easier to talk about the ideal world. This must have been President Bush's goal in November 2006 when he announced that he would divert existing family planning funds to expand his abstinence-only education initiatives. It makes a nice sound bite but a dangerous policy. Too much of what's taught in the abstinence-only curricula that the president supports is a fantasy. It might seem crazy, but students all over the United States are taught that condoms don't make sex safer and that HIV can be transmitted through casual contact in gym class. Research has documented that students in some abstinence-only programs are taught that touching another person's genitals "can result in pregnancy"[8]; that "there's no such thing as 'safe' or 'safer' sex"; that "loneliness, embarrassment, substance abuse, and personal disappointment"[9] can be avoided by being abstinent until marriage; and, according to one training manual for an abstinence-only program, that HIV can be transmitted through sweat and tears.[10]

As absurd as abstinence-only education is, too many politicians shy away from this issue completely, thereby failing to stand up for the truth. Here, political correctness works against the left and for the right. Talking about educating kids about contraception is dicey. You run the risk of being branded a "liberal" purveyor of loose morals or being accused of encouraging teen sex.

Members of Congress and responsible family planning organizations don't peddle sex among teens. We encourage abstinence *and* know that we can't stop there if we want to prevent teen pregnancies, abortions, and the transmission of diseases in the real world.

Too often, though, too many are afraid of either offending parents who are squeamish about thinking realistically or being targeted by

A cornerstone of the abstinence-only curricula has been misleading, incomplete information about human papillomavirus (HPV). In a small percentage of infected females, HPV, the most common sexually transmitted infective agent, can trigger cervical cancer, which kills 5,000 American women a year. While condoms substantially reduce transmission of HPV, they are not as effective against HPV as they are against other STDs.[11]

Many abstinence-only programs ignore the benefits of condom use and fail to teach that having regular Pap tests can detect precancerous cells, enabling doctors to remove them before cervical cancer develops. Instead, they play on the fear of cancer to deter any sexual activity among the unwed. Some right-wing organizations opposed FDA approval of the HPV vaccine. In effect, these groups were saying, "Thanks, but no thanks" to the first-ever cancer vaccine, believing it would diminish the fear factor of the abstinence-only curriculum by eliminating the risk of cervical cancer.

The Family Research Council's president, Tony Perkins, was explicit. He said that the vaccine "sends the wrong message.... This vaccine will be marketed to a segment of the population that should be getting a message about abstinence."[12]

Fortunately, the objections to the HPV vaccine proved too extreme for even the FDA, which approved it in 2006. Now, we have to fight to make sure that every young woman, wherever she lives, has access to it.

attack organizations that twist taking a responsible position into promoting a perverted agenda.

The result is social conservatives driving *their* agenda. In November 2006, President Bush announced that he would divert existing family planning funds to expand his abstinence-only education initiatives to women as old as 29.

You call this progress?

• Beginning in 1996, schools became eligible for federal funding only if their sex education curriculum was strictly limited, teaching that sex outside of marriage is likely to have harmful effects and refraining from discussing the health benefits of contraception, including condoms.[13]

• Eleven of the 13 commonly used abstinence-education programs contained "major errors and distortions" about health and medical information.[14]

• A meta-analysis of results from five abstinence-only programs found an increase in the number of pregnancies among the female partners of boys in the programs.[15]

• Eighty-six percent of the reduction in teen pregnancies between 1995 and 2002 was attributable to increased contraceptive use by sexually active teens.[16]

• During the Bush administration, federal funding for abstinence-only education more than doubled.[17]

EMERGENCY CONTRACEPTION EMERGENCY

When she was 19, Katie Smith moved to Indiana to attend college. Shortly after arriving, she went to a local pharmacy to have her prescription for a birth control pill filled.

"I'm sorry, young lady," huffed the pharmacist. "I don't fill these. I mean, I don't hand out pills so young girls can have sex. If you have a husband, which I doubt, bring him in with you next time, and you can have the pills."

"Why does he get to make assumptions about women and refuse to give them medicine a doctor says they can have?" asked Katie in recounting her experience. "I'll bet he fills Viagra prescriptions. I doubt any guy has to bring in a wife before getting those pills."[18] (The irony is that Katie wasn't even having sex. Her gynecologist had prescribed birth control pills to curb what Katie called "horrible periods.")

But the anger Katie felt because of the inappropriate actions of a rude, sexist pharmacist pales in comparison with the pain experienced by Michelle, who didn't want me to include her last name. In the summer of 2005, after extensive counseling and consultation, Michelle made the difficult decision to end her 12-year marriage. On her first night in a new apartment with her children, her husband showed up drunk—as was not uncommon.

After 20 minutes of arguing, he beat and raped her. His parting words were, "I know you won't leave me if you're pregnant."

Michelle was awake all night crying. Tears streamed down her bleeding, injured face. In the morning, she weighed her options and called her doctor, who urged her to call the police and report the rape. She refused for the sake of the kids.

"I didn't know what it would do to the boys if [they knew] their father was a rapist," she said. "They [were] already losing so much. . . . And if he lost his job, he couldn't pay child support. . . . I couldn't support the kids."

Her doctor agreed to call in a prescription for emergency contraception (EC).

Relieved and telling herself that it would all work out, Michelle drove to the local pharmacy, only to find that they didn't stock EC. So she headed to Wal-Mart.

When she handed the prescription to the Wal-Mart pharmacist, he looked at her with contempt. "We don't carry this," he scoffed as he shoved the prescription back to her.

Michelle asked if he could order it.

He started to walk away, Michelle told me. Then, "from about 50 feet away, he turns and says loud enough for practically everyone in the damn store to hear, 'I mean we don't kill babies. You'll have to find someone else to do that for you.'"

During our fight to *get emergency contraception (EC) approved for over-the-counter purchase, Congressman Steve Israel (D-NY) gave me a call. He told me that a pharmacist at a Pathmark pharmacy in his district on Long Island had refused to fill a prescription for EC and had not referred the medical professional calling in the prescription to another pharmacist at the store or to another pharmacy. The American Pharmaceutical Association's ethics policy endorses the "refusal clause" that gives pharmacists the right to conscientious refusal to fill a prescription, but it also mandates that they ensure the patient has access to legally prescribed medications by giving the prescription to another pharmacist at the same store or referring the patient to another pharmacy.*

Several states have passed legislation legalizing "refusal clauses" for pharmacists. These laws exempt pharmacists from obeying certain laws if doing so would force them to violate their strongly held religious beliefs. Shortly after the Roe v.

The sanctimonious Wal-Mart pharmacist didn't understand the product. Emergency contraception is just that—contraception. It's essentially a high dose of a birth control pill. Unlike mifepristone, a pill that nonsurgically terminates existing pregnancies, EC *prevents* pregnancy by blocking ovulation, fertilization, or implantation before it occurs. If a woman is already pregnant, EC will not affect the embryo. If she's not, she won't get pregnant.

Michelle called 13 other pharmacies—some were friendly, some scornful. None carried the drug; those who offered to order it couldn't get it in time. Michelle called her doctor, sobbing uncontrollably. Just before 5 p.m., he knocked on her door with the medication in hand.

Wade decision, Congress passed the Church Amendment, which gave individuals and medical facilities the right to decline to perform abortions based on their religious and ethical beliefs. Within five years, the majority of states adopted similar clauses.

At a press conference that we held outside the Pathmark, I discussed a bill I had introduced called the Access to Birth Control Act. The bill would require that if a pharmacist had a personal objection to filling a legal prescription for a drug or device, the pharmacy would have to ensure that the prescription was filled without delay by another pharmacist who did not have a personal objection. It would also ensure that if a prescription drug that the pharmacy normally carried was not in stock, the drug would be ordered without delay.

Though Pathmark denied the incident had ever taken place, you can be sure that after our press conference, no similar incident will happen at that store again.

"I didn't ask him where he got it. I didn't even care. I was crying too hard at that point, and I just wanted the whole thing to be over. I took the medicine, drank a glass of water, and thanked him over and over," said Michelle.[19]

Experiences like Kate's and Michelle's are, sadly, not unique. That's why I was so heartened in December 2003, when an advisory panel of the FDA, after concurring unanimously that it would be safe to do so based on the scientific evidence, endorsed by a vote of 23 to 4 the idea of making Plan B, a brand of EC, available over the counter.

But my excitement waned as I began to suspect that the Bush administration would yet again put politics in the way of the science behind reproductive rights. In January 2004, I wrote a letter signed by 75 colleagues to the Bush-appointed then-FDA commissioner Mark McClellan (Scott's brother), urging him to heed the panel's recommendation.

Despite the letter and the recommendation of its own expert panel, sure enough, on May 6, 2004, the FDA announced that it would delay its decision on the manufacturer's application to make Plan B available over the counter.

Six days after the FDA said no to Plan B, Representative Joseph Crowley (D-NY) and I, along with 14 Democratic cosponsors, introduced the Science Over Politics Act to compel the FDA commissioner to review the decision on Plan B and affirm that it was not politically influenced, that it was based on sound science, and that it conformed to FDA precedent and procedure.

Introducing the bill was a tactic undertaken within a broader strategy. Its merit notwithstanding, there was no way that the Republican leadership would pass a bill requiring a commissioner to affirm that his decision was not politically motivated, especially since it *was* politically motivated. Sometimes, it's worth it to introduce legislation that you know will have great difficulty passing in the short term. The bill and the publicity it generates can be a rallying cry for the cause you are championing.

In this case, to our pleasant surprise, the torrent of advocacy in favor of reproductive rights paved the way for passage of a form of the bill—an amendment that was incorporated into an agricultural appropriations bill. The amendment was not as complete as the original bill (it is rare to get something passed in its original form, especially when your party is in the minority, as mine was back then), but the Sound Science Amendment, which I introduced with Representative Henry Waxman (D-CA) was designed to require the FDA to use scientific standards, not political considerations, in making the determination about over-the-counter status for contraceptives.

The case that I had been making got a huge boost in August 2005, when the director of the FDA's Office of Women's Health, Dr. Susan Wood, resigned. "I have spent the last 15 years working to ensure that science informs good health policy decisions. I can no longer serve as staff when scientific and clinical evidence, fully evaluated and recommended for approval by the senior professional staff here, has been overruled," she said. After quitting the FDA, Wood continued to build support for EC by speaking across the nation, including at a forum that I organized.

Also in August 2005, the FDA announced that it would miss another promised deadline for deciding whether Plan B could be sold over the counter.

In November, together with other House members, I introduced another bill—the Plan B for Plan B Act—to require the FDA to rule on Plan B within 30 days.

A few weeks later, the nonpartisan Government Accountability Office released the results of a study that found that before the FDA's scientists had completed their review, Stephen Galson, a political appointee who was then the acting director of the FDA Center for Drug Evaluation and Research, had told them that the application for over-the-counter status would be denied.[20]

The supposed rationale for delaying approval was crumbling all around the FDA.

While the Plan B drama was playing out at the FDA, the Department of Justice (DOJ) joined in the administration's seemingly systemic opposition to reproductive rights in general and EC in particular.

Early drafts of new DOJ guidelines for how hospitals should treat rape victims suggested that doctors tell patients about EC since some religiously affiliated hospitals won't even inform rape survivors of EC, which has prompted progressive states like Massachusetts to pass laws requiring them to do so. But apparently, decision makers at DOJ—and presumably the White House—believed it was improper to help a woman avoid bearing her rapist's child. So the mention of EC was deleted from the guidelines.

A month and a 95-member-signed protest letter later, I showed up at the DOJ hearing on the new guidelines, held at a downtown Washington, D.C., hotel, to testify. I was the only member of Congress there. As far as I know, I was also the only aspiring witness who was prevented from testifying, prevented from submitting written testimony, and commanded to leave by

Then, in March, the FDA nominated a new commissioner, Dr. Andrew von Eschenbach, who needed Senate approval to take his post. Senators Hillary Rodham Clinton and Patty Murray (D-WA) vowed to block the nomination until the FDA made a final ruling on Plan B.

This was the final, successful step. In July, the FDA said it would reconsider the application for women ages 18 and over. Less than a month later, it approved over-the-counter access for adults, although girls ages 17 and under still would need a prescription.

a DOJ official who threatened to have security haul me out if I didn't go quietly.

The incident exposed the hearing for what it was: a cynical formality constructed to muzzle an opposing viewpoint. As I wrote to then–US attorney general Alberto Gonzales after the hearing, "Each and every viewpoint should be respected at public hearings, particularly when they concern a topic so important as the health of rape victims. [The] stubborn resistance [of the hearing's organizers] to [my airing] the opposing viewpoint suggests that they are, in fact, embarrassed by the lack of health options they are willing to give victims."

Not surprisingly, Mr. Gonzales never responded.

In March 2005, exactly a month after the hearing, I introduced the Best Help for Rape Victims Act, which would mandate that DOJ include in the guidelines language about informing victims about the purpose and availability of EC.

It is still not the law of the land.

It was an amazing victory engineered by countless people and organizations—a true testament to the possibility of changing things when politicians, organizations, and citizens team up and take action to accomplish what's right.

- EC can reduce a woman's chance of conceiving by 89 percent.[21]

University of Massachusetts, Amherst, sophomore Linda For-man heard that a pharmacist at a local CVS had refused to fill birth control prescriptions. Then Linda, who was the head of Vox: Students for Choice at UMass, a student-run organization affiliated with Planned Parenthood, learned about a larger problem: Wal-Mart's policy of not carrying emergency contra-ception. Linda gathered together members of Vox and other like-minded student groups in the area. Thirty student and community members of four different organizations stood in the mud outside a Wal-Mart in Hadley, Massachusetts, chant-ing and holding signs.

Some motorists who pulled over to ask questions were sur-prised to learn that EC was not mifepristone, which terminates existing pregnancies. A few people even got out of their cars and joined the protest.

The media ate it up. NBC and ABC affiliates covered the story, along with local radio stations and newspapers. It snow-balled from there. Planned Parenthood organized similar events throughout the state and across the country.

Meanwhile, Vox and other concerned citizens throughout the state collected signatures and lobbied members of the Massachusetts state legislature. On Valentine's Day 2006, the Massachusetts Board of Pharmacy voted to require Wal-Mart

• The sooner you take EC after intercourse, the more effective it is; its effectiveness wanes sharply after 72 hours.[22]

• Studies have found that widespread use of EC could prevent an estimated 1.7 million unintended pregnancies and between 600,000 and 800,000 abortions each year.[23]

to stock EC in its pharmacies. A year to the day after the rally Linda had spearheaded, Wal-Mart agreed to carry EC at all of its stores.

Members of Congress have the standing to expect answers when we write letters or take stands. Linda had no such platform. All she had was her passion and some like-minded friends whom she inspired and led. Linda, whom I hired after graduation, succeeded where many members of Congress had failed— in trying to get Wal-Mart to change anything about the way it does business.

I remembered something Gloria Steinem said to me over breakfast one day. She and I were discussing activism among young women, and I lamented that young women today aren't as openly active on the right to choose as our generation had been, even though they face a great risk of losing that right. But overall, Gloria's assessment was upbeat. "Young women may not be as concerned about choice as we were, probably because they grew up with that right and we didn't," she told me. "But boy, are they angry about the lack of sex education in schools and pharmacists giving them lectures and not filling prescriptions for birth control."

Linda proved her right.

WOLF IN SHEEP'S CLOTHING

The Title X Family Planning Program is a 37-year-old federal program that is the primary source of funding for the Planned Parenthood Federation of America and just about all other reputable family planning programs in the country.

More and more federal funds are going to fund crisis pregnancy centers (CPCs). CPCs are sprouting up around the country, often in locations very close to Planned Parenthood clinics or other family planning centers. A large majority of CPCs are what they say they are—religious organizations that help women with unplanned pregnancies find an alternative to abortion. But some are not what they seem at all. They target "abortion-vulnerable" women and use deceptive advertising practices to give the appearance that they provide a variety of reproductive services, including family planning and abortion care. They even fly flags using the same color scheme as Planned Parenthood and advertise in phone books under "abortion services." Once a woman is inside, CPCs don't offer her objective advice or support, nor do they perform abortions as is often suggested in their advertising. Instead, they offer shock and fear.[24] Women might hear misinformation about health risks—like "abortion causes breast cancer"—or be offered prenatal care only if they sign adoption papers. At some CPCs, women who have received the free prenatal care that's advertised have had the assistance cut off after 24 weeks, when abortion becomes illegal in most states.[25] There are even reported cases of CPC employees lying about positive pregnancy tests so that a woman won't realize she is pregnant until it is too late to have a legal abortion.[26]

A college student we'll call Tracy had an experience with a CPC that is all too common. When she thought she might be pregnant, she saw an ad for AAA Crisis Pregnancy Center in her college newspaper. It advertised free pregnancy tests. Because she was low on money, she went there. While she

Shortly after the midterm elections, Dr. Eric Keroack was appointed to be the deputy assistant secretary at the Department of Health and Human Services' Office of Population Affairs. The job includes overseeing the Title X Family Planning Program, which is the primary source of family planning funding in the country. Keroack, an obstetrician-gynecologist opposed to sex education, had previously served as medical director at A Woman's Concern (AWC), a nonprofit organization that runs CPCs in Massachusetts.[27] As soon as I heard about Keroack's appointment, my stomach sank.

AWC is more straightforward about its services and convictions than some CPCs are, but its honesty is chilling in its own way. Its position on contraception? "The crass commercialization and distribution of birth control is demeaning to women, degrading of human sexuality and adverse to human health and happiness." AWC's position on EC? Staff and volunteers must "not distribute birth control drugs or devices."[28]

As I considered Keroak's record, I looked back at the letter affirming the president's support of contraception. It stated that the administration "faithfully executes laws establishing Federal programs to provide contraception and family planning services ... [including the] Title X Family Planning Program."

That's when it occurred to me that there is more than one meaning of "executes."

Keroack resigned shortly after his confirmation amid allegations of insurance fraud in his private practice. Susan Orr, another antichoice activist, has been nominated to head the office.

was waiting for the results of her test, Tracy was shown a graphic film "about" abortion called *The Silent Scream*. When the test came back positive, she told AAA's "counselor" that despite the manipulative images she'd seen in the film, she still wanted an abortion. The counselor responded that she would regret it, develop psychological problems, and possibly become sterile.

Rattled, Tracy headed for the exit. She was handed baby clothes on her way out the door.

In March 2006, with the support of Planned Parenthood, NARAL Pro-Choice America, the National Abortion Federation, the American Civil Liberties Union, and 10 cosponsors, I introduced the Stop Deceptive Advertising for Women's Services Act to enforce truth-in-advertising standards for reproductive health centers. The bill would make it illegal to deceptively advertise that an organization offers abortion services when in fact it doesn't.

- More than 4.8 million American women rely on Title X funding to meet their reproductive health needs.

- Sixty-eight percent of them live below the poverty level.

- In total, publicly subsidized family planning services, of which Title X is the core, prevented more than 20 million unintended pregnancies and more than 9 million abortions.[29]

PARTIAL ABORTION RIGHTS

I fundamentally believe that a woman has a right to control her own body; that she should be able to decide whether or not to terminate a pregnancy with her doctor and her loved ones rather than having the government make that decision for her. But other people arrive at that position because of the circumstances of their lives.

Mary Dorothy Line and her husband were thrilled to be pregnant. But their joy turned to horror when they learned at 19 weeks that the fetus had hydrocephalus—too much fluid cushioning the brain from the skull, which results in the failure of the brain to develop. As practicing Catholics, they and their family prayed for a miracle—and never thought about an abortion. But on their next doctor's visit, they learned that the case was advanced and that the fetus had no chance of survival. The only question was whether it would die in utero or just after birth. Death in utero could have caused hemorrhaging and possibly hysterectomy. Natural labor could have caused rupturing of the cervix and Mary's uterus. So she had what the antichoicers call a "partial birth abortion," in which the fetus has to be partially delivered before it could be aborted.

At a 1996 press conference with President Clinton just after he vetoed the so-called Partial Birth Abortion Act, Mary said, "I thank God every day that I had this safe medical option available to me, especially now that I am pregnant again. . . . I thank God for President Clinton. . . . [He] listened to us and protected families like ours by vetoing legislation that would hurt so many people."

But Congress passed the act and President Bush signed it into law in 2003. The act was purported to ban only later-stage abortions, but its wording was made deliberately vague in order to make it potentially applicable as early as 12 weeks into a pregnancy. It is often carried out when the fetus is not viable and/or the health or life of the mother is at risk. It was the first federal law ever passed to outlaw a specific abortion procedure without an exception for preserving the life or health of the woman, which should be guaranteed under *Roe v. Wade.*

District and appeals courts in three separate states struck down the ban when it was challenged by the nonprofit Center for Reproductive Rights and Planned Parenthood. On November 8, 2006—the day after Democrats' victorious midterm elections—the Supreme Court heard oral arguments on the act. They were going to decide once and for all if the law passed constitutional muster.

In 2000,[30] in a decision written by Justice Sandra Day O'Connor, the Supreme Court had struck down a "partial birth abortion" law passed in Nebraska on the grounds that there was no exception for life and health of the mother.

In 2003, Congress passed a remarkably similar law that had no exception. After Justice O'Connor retired, I had a conversation with her in which I said: "You gave a blueprint to Congress about what legislation needed to include to pass constitutional muster. I thought Congress would follow your blueprint." She seemed to me to agree.

Obviously, rather than revising the bill to address Justice O'Connor's

"Partial birth abortion" is a made-for-politics name that has no accepted medical meaning. Congressman Charles T. Canady (R-FL) created the term in 1995 to shock and to mislead Americans into believing that the procedure covered only late-term abortions of viable fetuses. This is simply not the case.

The most common abortion procedure is dilation and evacuation, or D&E. The medical term for what the right refers to as a partial birth abortion is actually intact D&E. Anti-choicers claim that intact D&E is never medically necessary; that a woman who is legally entitled to an abortion can always use another procedure that is just as safe. This also is not the case. Sometimes, doctors set out to perform a regular D&E but must resort to intact D&E because it proves to be the only way to protect a woman's fertility and health. Standard D&E procedures have the potential to morph into intact D&Es as early as 12 weeks into pregnancy. A representative from the American concerns, the Republican Congress counted on a change in the composition of the Supreme Court to get their restrictive language upheld. That's why I wasn't surprised when, with two conservative newcomers, Chief Justice John Roberts and Justice Samuel Alito, the Court agreed to take the case. Despite victories in six lower courts, I was not confident that this case before this Court would yield a seventh win. The scientific evidence hadn't changed after previous Supreme Court rulings. The precedents hadn't changed. The only real change was in the composition of the Court. In my mind, it was not the case but rather the Court that was on trial.

I wanted to see for myself whether this new Court was willing to affirm women's rights or intent upon gutting them. On November 8, the

College of Obstetricians and Gynecologists said that intact D&E procedures in some cases are the safest way to avert, among other things, perforation of the uterus, infertility, hemorrhage, the spread of malignant cancer throughout a woman's body, and damage to vital organs when a woman has a disease.

Congress's opposition to this procedure was full of politics and almost devoid of medicine. At the root of the controversy is the fact that intact D&E is more upsetting to many people than the in utero procedure. But that objection is about emotion, not about health care and the sound practice of medicine. As long as abortion is legal, the health and safety of the mother must trump emotion and politics. Opposing a doctor's right to make the best medical decisions for a woman who chooses abortion is the same as opposing choice itself. Whatever brand names opponents give to their bans, the truth is that they are banning choice.

morning after a joyous celebration of the Democrats reclaiming control of the House, I sat in the courtroom and looked out on the Court's two new faces, Alito and Roberts. Nothing could have been more sobering. I had virtually no hope that Alito would vote to strike down the ban. At a lunch we both attended, I asked him if he thought *Roe v. Wade* was settled law. Just as he had at his Senate confirmation hearings, he didn't answer and politely demurred. "Always remember the women," I suggested as he left.

Roberts, however, had declared *Roe v. Wade* "settled law" at his confirmation hearings. He was the potential swing vote for women's rights. All eyes, including mine, were trained on him.

As I sat there, I was struck, as I always am, by the demographics of the group that rules on how to regulate a woman's reproductive system. Only one of them had her own rights on trial.

The votes of individual justices can be unpredictable. Still, as I sat watching the arguments, I got the impression that the four justices who had joined O'Connor in 2000—Stephen Breyer, John Paul Stevens, Ruth Bader Ginsburg, and David Souter—were right where they had been.

Antonin Scalia chimed in only a few times during the oral arguments. Alito and Clarence Thomas might as well have been sitting next to me; they were spectators who spoke not a word. But it didn't matter; I knew how the three of them would vote.

Roberts seemed antagonistic toward the lawyers representing the Center for Reproductive Rights but did not challenge the lawyer—the United States solicitor general, Paul Clement, a Bush appointee—supporting the ban. Not a good sign.

The tea leaves, however, seemed to offer one last hope: Anthony Kennedy. He challenged the solicitor general and expressed concern that the ban could make doctors vulnerable to prosecution.[31] But he was equally challenging to the other side. And he had sided with the minority in the Court's previous decision on the same issue.

Five months later, my worst fears were realized. The Court disavowed the precedent it had set just six years earlier, overturned the lower courts' decisions, and upheld the abortion ban.

It was one of the darkest days for reproductive rights in a generation or more. The decision served as a stark reminder that President Bush's appointees to our courts are not interested in consistency or legal precedent. They are able and willing to eviscerate women's rights without a blink of the eye. As Center for Reproductive Rights president Nancy Northrup put it, "Nothing has changed since the 2000 decision. No new facts have emerged. The only change has been in the makeup of the Court."

The appalling, legally flawed, and regressive decision was a clarion call warning a new generation of women that the reproductive rights that some of them take for granted are surviving today on the razor's edge.

I kept and publicized a scorecard of anti-choice actions after the Republicans gained the majority in the House in 1995. By July 2005, when I last issued an update, the total had reached 176. Federal employees had lost coverage for abortion in their health insurance plans. Women service members had been banned from having abortions at overseas military bases, even if they intended to pay for them themselves. While they were overseas protecting our rights and freedoms, Congress was at home stripping them of theirs. Just prior to the 2006 election, both the House and the Senate passed bills making escorting a minor across state lines to have an abortion a crime, although they weren't able to reconcile the differences in the bills before the session ended, preventing the attempt from becoming law.[32]

HOW TO STEAL $34 MILLION

Mary Solio was born and raised in a tiny village in Kenya. She was 15 when her father told her she would be married off to a 40-year-old man. She begged him not to do it, but to no avail. One friend told her she should escape to the nearest town to seek refuge and continue her education.

Two days before her wedding, Mary made a break for it at dawn. Her father and relatives of the "groom" chased her down, stripped her naked, and beat her. She was dragged back to the village, where she was beaten "like an animal," then returned to her "fiancé's" home.

"I begged my father," Mary said. "I cried to him. But he told me that he had married off many girls, and I was the only one who wanted to let him down.

"In my husband's home, every day I was fighting because he forced me to sleep with him, but I did not accept him because he was so much older than me," she said. Her husband's sister was assigned to follow her wherever she went to make sure she didn't try to run away again. But Mary gave her the slip and made the marathon-length journey to the closest village, Narok, fearing animal attacks in the forest all the way.

Mary was lucky, because Narok has a home for girls escaping forced early marriage and female circumcision. It is called Tasaru Ntomonok, which means "to rescue the woman." Tasaru Ntomonok is run by a survivor of female genital mutilation, Agnes Pareiyo. There, Mary received food, shelter, and a lawyer, who went to court to prevent her family from taking her back home after they tracked her down.[33]

Mary is not alone in battling customs that deny women fundamental human rights. In some regions, girls marry at an average age of as young as 11. In Ethiopia and some areas of West Africa, some girls get married as early as age 8 or 9.[34] In parts of Africa, pregnancy is the number one cause of death for girls and women of childbearing age. Women also die of infection due to female genital mutilation, which 130 million women and girls have undergone.[35] When their husbands die, some women and girls cannot inherit their property. They are either sold off as slaves or wives or forced out of their homes, winding up with only their bodies to sell to support their families.

In India, things are just as bad. I once asked the US ambassador to India, Frank G. Wisner Jr., what America could do to help the country. Given its widespread poverty, I expected him to say something related to economic development. To my surprise, he said we needed to support family planning. He told me that people line up for blocks to be seen at family planning clinics. Lack of access to birth control is a major reason that India has four times as many people as we do and so many of those people are poor. Infant mortality is high, and according to 2000 World Health Organization data, 540 of every 100,000 women who gave birth died doing so, largely for lack of appropriate health care. In comparison, in the United States, that figure was 17.[36]

Tragic, you are probably thinking. But what can we do about these intractable problems in far-flung places?

The United Nations Population Fund (UNFPA) is the world's largest multilateral provider of family planning programs and funding. The organization provides pre- and postnatal care as well as helping to make delivery safer for women and girls in more than 140 countries. It also promotes contraception and safe-sex practices to limit unplanned pregnancies and the spread of HIV.

To do this lifesaving work, UNFPA depends on funding from the United States. In every year since 2002, Congress has done its part by approving and appropriating $34 million for the fund.

But every year, President Bush has blocked it.

The estimated death toll of our president's refusal to send funds to UNFPA exceeds the entire population of New Mexico. In the developing world, $34 million goes a long way. Had that money gone into contraceptive commodities, it could have saved nearly 500,000 lives.[37]

In opposing UNFPA, the president is doing the fundamentalist right's bidding and selling poor women around the world straight down the river. The Christian Coalition of America has called UNFPA a "radical pro-abortion organization"[38] and accused it of supporting the forced abortion and sterilization program in China.

In fact, UNFPA neither supports nor funds abortions anywhere in the world. (If it did, Congress wouldn't bother to appropriate funds for it, because it would already be illegal under the Hyde Amendment, which forbids the use of federal funds for abortion.)

On his first full day in office in 1993, President Clinton issued an executive order lifting the Global Gag Rule. It was a courageous act that did away with a terrible policy.

The Global Gag Rule dictates that international health organizations that provide abortions or, in most cases,[39] even advise women about the option of abortion are ineligible for US foreign assistance. In America, censoring doctors and health professionals would be unconstitutional under the First Amendment. But we don't always export the version of democracy that Americans enjoy at home.

Then, in 1999, the Clinton administration took a step backward. In order to resolve an impasse over paying dues to the United Nations—the president wanted to pay what we owed, and congressional Republicans were blocking it—with the stroke of a pen, the president reinstated the gag rule.

Though I support funding the United Nations as much as anyone (its headquarters, after all, are in my district), I joined with women's groups, activists, and others in feeling enraged and betrayed.

No one opposes China's one-child-per-family policy more strongly or publicly than UNFPA. In fact, UNFPA restricts its programs in China to counties where the quotas and targets imposed by the single-child policy have been removed. An investigative team from the US State Department found no evidence of UNFPA supporting China's policy and recommended that the United States restore its contribution to the fund.[40]

In contrast, no one is wimpier about urging China to abandon its single-child policy than President Bush in his face-to-face meetings with Chinese leaders. I've never seen a news report noting that the president or

We endeavored to raise consciousness on the issue by sending letters and petitions and holding press conferences—all the tried-and-true tactics of political persuasion. Then, instead of additional vociferous outrage, we tried a new tactic. Every week, one women's organization or advocate would send a bouquet of flowers to President Clinton's White House deputy chief of staff, Steve Richetti. It was my job to send the first one. I deliberated over what color to send. Red seemed to have the wrong connotations. Pink seemed too docile. I opted for yellow tulips.

I don't know whether Richetti found this kill-him-with-kindness gesture unsettling or humorous. All I know is that it was part of a winning strategy—Nancy Pelosi and others worked out a compromise with the White House to allow the Global Gag Rule to expire.

Who said flower power is dead?

Unfortunately, the victory was short-lived: President Bush reinstated the ban on his first day in office in 2001.

The knee-jerk and irrational opposition to contraception is not just damaging family planning programs. It is also diminishing the effectiveness of the Bush administration's critically important initiative aimed at eradicating HIV/AIDS in developing countries around the world, a goal that's shared with UNFPA. In 2003, President Bush announced the President's Emergency Plan for AIDS Relief (PEPFAR), pledging to commit $15 billion over five years to address the HIV/AIDS epidemic in developing countries—a stunning announcement given that HIV/AIDS prevention and treatment was never high on the list of conservative Republican priorities. The administration dubbed the prevention program the "ABC" approach to HIV/AIDS prevention—abstinence, be faithful, and correct and consistent condom use.

In April 2006, a study by the nonpartisan Government Accountability Office found that in practice, ABC tends to emphasize A and B. The study concluded that AB without C has not only proved ineffective but has actually been harmful to HIV/AIDS prevention because it funnels money away from proven programs that emphasize condoms.

Secretary of State Condoleezza Rice or any other administration official raised the issue directly with the Chinese.

The real obstacle to UNFPA isn't China. It's the same anti-reproductive rights ideology that is doing so much damage at home. For example, when Congressman Christopher Smith (R-NJ) demanded on the House floor in 1999 that UNFPA funding be discontinued, he cited a report by the fringe anti–family planning group the Population Research Institute that stated that contraception leads to "increased promiscuity, adultery, and prostitution, and to perverse sexual practices, including homosexual practices."[41]

The idea that the US government is leaving millions of women and girls for dead has made UNFPA funding a top priority for me. I have led the bipartisan effort in Congress each year since 1999 to obtain the $34 million in assistance for UNFPA. But in 2006, for the fifth year in a row,

Fortunately, the women President Bush *has abandoned have not been forgotten by millions of Americans. After President Bush first stripped funding from UNFPA in 2002, two ordinary-but-extraordinary American women previously unknown to each other and living hundreds of miles apart both decided to take action.*

When the two activists—Jane Roberts of Redlands, California, and Lois Abraham of Santa Fe, New Mexico—met, they came up with a novel and brilliant idea: solicit $1 donations from 34 million people to make up for the funding denied by the president. Jane and Lois founded the nonprofit group 34 Million Friends of UNFPA (www.34millionfriends.org).

I asked Jane how she and Lois overcame the million-and-one setbacks that happen with organizing any movement. "I am quite stubborn about this because I actually want to make a small difference in the world and to leave it a better place when I depart," she said. "So I do not get discouraged, and I continue to be joyfully relentless in searching for 34 million friends of the women of the world."

Jane has chronicled her and Lois's journey from outrage to activism in a book named after the organization. As of November 2007, 34 Million Friends had raised almost $3.6 million in individual donations.

the Bush administration ignored the facts and invoked a law that allows the president to withhold funding from any organization that supports a program of forced abortion or sterilization.

Finally, I offered a compromise. To avoid the controversy surrounding contraception, I proposed devoting the $34 million solely to UNFPA's Campaign to End Fistula.

If you've never heard of fistula, it's because it's an obstetric problem that's so easy to prevent and repair that it's almost unheard of in the United States. Yet obstetric fistula affects 100,000 women every year worldwide, most of them in Africa. Usually a result of prolonged labor, fistula occurs when the descending baby's head pressing against the mother's pelvic bone kills the delicate vaginal tissue and leaves a hole through which urine and feces pass uncontrollably. Untreated, the condition lasts a lifetime. The baby is usually stillborn. Many women who survive obstetric fistula are abandoned by their husbands, stigmatized by society, and forced to spend the rest of their lives begging.

But my compromise was rejected, too. Who would strike down an effort to fight a condition that kills thousands of babies every year and condemns their mothers to poverty and degradation? It turns out that the biggest opponents of my compromise were those who pass themselves off as pro-life.

You call this progress?

• The loss of $34 million per year since 2002, the amount that the United States owes UNFPA, may have led to
  • up to 12 million unwanted pregnancies
  • 4.8 million induced abortions
  • 28,200 maternal deaths
  • 462,000 infant and child deaths[42]

• One UNFPA family planning project increased both gynecological and prenatal-care visits in its coverage area by 50 percent.[43]

Take-Action Guide

A Womb of Our Own

The assault on reproductive rights and the backsliding it has wrought has been a call to arms for women's rights groups. Numerous organizations today maintain that vigilance by providing extensive resources on many or all aspects of reproductive rights. They'll put you to work at the grassroots level and in the political domain. Each may have a specific forte, but all offer a wide range of opportunities for activism and involvement. I encourage you to explore any or all of them to find the opportunities for making a difference that suit you best.

1. Help make sure that comprehensive, accurate sex education is available to all schoolchildren.

• **Lobby your school district to reject federal funds tied to abstinence-only education programs, and learn what sex and sexuality information your schools provide to students.** Typically, the only parents who attend their children's sex education or abstinence-only education classes are from the fundamentalist right. Members of the "silent majority" need to show up for class, too. The Sexuality Information and Education Council of the United States provides state-by-state information that can help you understand sex ed in your state and, at www.siecus.org/policy/legislative/legis0000. html, inform you of any legislative issues on the horizon that can affect what kind of information your children receive.

• **Urge your members of Congress to support the Responsible Education about Life (REAL) Act,** which would establish the first-ever federal program to fund comprehensive and medically accurate sex education. See www.siecus.org/policy/legislative/legis0000.html for up-to-date information on this and other legislation.

• **Educate your kids.** Advocates for Youth is an organization that helps ensure that young people have access to comprehensive health information—and sex education in particular—along with the psychological skills to navigate through the decisions they'll face. It has a Web site section devoted to parents' resources for sex education, including tips for talking about everything from the birds and the bees to contraception. Their abstinence-only education Web page, at www. advocatesforyouth.org/abstinenceonly.htm, has up-to-date information on the state of American sex education and how to improve it.

2. Prevent government laws and regulations from standing in the way of a woman's or girl's freedom to choose for herself.

• **Urge your members of Congress to support the Compassionate Assistance for Rape Emergencies Act** that would make it a requirement that rape victims be offered EC in the emergency room.

• **Find practical information on where to get EC,** such as which providers and pharmacies carry it, and how to advocate to make it universally available at www.not-2-late.com. Also see www. plannedparenthood.org/birth-control-pregnancy/emergency-contraception/getting-ec.htm

3. Fight to eradicate pharmacist refusal clauses that could prevent a woman or girl from purchasing contraception in a timely manner.

• **Urge your members of Congress to support my Access to Birth Control Act.** The bill ensures that if a pharmacist chooses not to dispense birth control pills (or any other legal medication), the pharmacy must have another pharmacist fill the prescription without delay.

• **Write to the parent company of your local drugstore if it carries EC and say it's earned your loyalty.** If it doesn't carry EC, say you've found another drugstore.

• **Support the Best Help for Rape Victims Act I've introduced,** which would mandate that DOJ include in the guidelines language about informing victims about the purpose and availability of EC.

4. Demand that health insurance companies offer comprehensive coverage of contraceptives.

• **Urge your members of Congress to support the Equity in Prescription Insurance and Contraceptive Coverage Act,** which would ensure that prescription birth control is covered at the same benefit level as other prescription drugs.

• **Urge your employers and schools to help.** Sample letters you can adapt and send to employers and schools to encourage them to choose employee health plans that include contraceptive coverage are available at www.covermypills.org. As of February 2006, 23 states required equitable coverage. Find out if yours is among them at www.covermypills.org/facts/statelaw. If not, go to www.ppfa.org for contact information for your local Planned Parenthood affiliate to find out how to get involved with its state campaigns to get coverage.

5. Work to keep abortions safe, legal, and accessible in the following ways.

• **Stay up to date on important legislation.** Write to your members of Congress and tell them to repeal the Partial Birth Abortion Ban. Do the same on the state level if your state has a similar law.

• **Work to make sure women and girls are never harassed or blocked from entering a family planning clinic that provides abortion services.** Due to a recent Supreme Court ruling that federal racketeering laws cannot be used to protect family planning clinics, the National Organization for Women (NOW) will be forced to revert to combating intrusive protestors on a clinic-by-clinic basis. You can help by volunteering at your local clinic and supporting NOW. Most Planned Parenthood clinics regularly need escort volunteers to walk patients safely through the clinic doors when protestors are on the streets outside. Call your local affiliate—you can find it at the national Web site, www.ppfa.org—to ask about volunteer opportunities.

• **Work to make sure that crisis pregnancy centers (CPCs) are subject to truth-in-advertising standards** and therefore are forbidden to misrepresent themselves as providers of abortion services in order to lure in women seeking abortion information. If you suspect a local health center is actually a CPC in disguise, the Feminist Majority Foundation Web site, www.feministcampus.org/know/sam/unit4.pdf, has an action plan that you can use to expose it with a team of just two to four people.

• **Urge your members of Congress to support the Stop Deceptive Advertising for Women's Services Act,** my bill that would enforce truth-in-advertising standards for reproductive centers. Check your local business telephone directory to see if any CPCs list themselves under "abortion services" or "abortion." If they do, report their false or deceptive advertising to the Better Business Bureau and directly to the directory publisher.

• **Oppose the federal Informed Choice Act,** which would allow nonprofit organizations to use federal money to purchase ultrasound equipment to provide "free examinations" for pregnant women.

While I am fully behind providing low-cost subsidized health care to pregnant women, this bill is a thinly disguised attempt to subsidize CPCs.

• **Oppose state-run license plate programs that funnel money to anti-choice organizations and give them advertising space on government property.** Florida's "Choose Life" license plates have generated $1.5 million for CPCs in that state.[44] Other states have similar programs, including South Carolina, Oklahoma, Mississippi, Alabama, Arkansas, Louisiana, Ohio, and Tennessee. Urge your state legislators to oppose or repeal similar state-level legislative measures. Michigan, Kansas, Minnesota, Missouri, Pennsylvania, Delaware, Louisiana, North Dakota, Texas, Virginia, Oklahoma, and California have all passed legislation granting tax dollars specifically to anti-choice CPCs. Contact your local NARAL Pro-Choice America affiliate to find out about legislation in your state. Work with NOW to get pro-choice license plates, as they did in Florida.

• **Vote as if your life, and the lives of your female family and friends, depend on it, because they just might.** The 2008 presidential election means everything. Educate yourself—know what the candidates stand for, what their voting records are, and how they plan to vote in the future—and vote for those whose views on reproductive rights most closely match your own. To stay active and informed about how you can advance the cause of choice between elections, monitor the Web sites of the best-known pro-choice organizations for news on legislation. The National Women's Law Center and the National Partnership for Women and Families have excellent resources as well. NARAL Pro-Choice America's Bush v. Choice blog at www.bushvchoice.com offers frequent entries about the erosion of reproductive rights. The National Abortion Federation also keeps up-to-the-minute notes on key issues in its blog at www.prochoice.org/blog. The Feminist Majority Foundation's Campus Program has what may be the largest pro-choice student network in the country. Its Web site is www.feministcampus.org.

8

★ ★ ★

A SEAT AT THE TABLE

"The stakes are much too high for government to be a spectator sport."

— BARBARA JORDAN

e need a New York woman to get the women out of the basement."

It was late at night on the floor of the House of Representatives in 1995, and I had no idea what Congresswoman Pat Schroeder was talking about.

It was the first session under Republican rule. My Democratic women colleagues and I were depressed. The onslaught of legislation rolling back long-held women's rights had already begun, and House Speaker Newt Gingrich (R-GA) was trying his darnedest to cripple all opposition.

We needed a morale booster. Pat Schroeder was drafting me for that role. My task was to introduce and get passed resolutions to move a 7½-ton statue of legendary women's suffragists from the Capitol basement to its rightful place in the grand Capitol Rotunda. The statue depicted the towering figures—Elizabeth Cady Stanton and Lucretia Mott—who had met at Seneca Falls, New York, in 1848 to kick off the women's movement, and

Susan B. Anthony, who met Stanton in 1851 and began working together to secure a woman's right to vote. It had been commissioned in 1920 upon passage of the 19th Amendment, which gave women the vote.

I had long idolized the suffragists for enduring ridicule, vilification, and incarceration to give women a voice in our democracy. In addition, Alice Paul, who was president of the National Woman Suffrage Association in 1920 and commissioned the statue, is family. She was the first cousin of my husband's grandmother, Florence Paul. According to Florence, Alice was the only member of the family who had ever had to be bailed out of jail. (My husband and I named our first daughter Christina Paul Maloney in honor of Alice.)

Moving the statue was wholly justified. The Rotunda had its share of great Americans—George Washington, Thomas Jefferson, Alexander Hamilton, and Martin Luther King Jr.—but no women.

The statue had been in the Rotunda before, for two days, after it was unveiled on Susan B. Anthony's birthday in 1921. Then Congress relegated it to a basement storage room in the Capitol Crypt. Adding insult to injury, the statue's inscription, "Woman, first denied a soul, then called mindless, now arisen, declared herself an entity to be reckoned," was soon erased for being "blasphemous"—though it never mentioned God.

Seventy-five years later, I learned that the more things change, the more they stay the same. Though we recruited a moderate Republican woman, Maryland's Connie Morella, and two sympathetic senators, John Warner (R-VA) and Ted Stevens (R-AK) as sponsors, the resolutions were never brought to the floor of either chamber.

In the next session of Congress, we reintroduced the resolution to move the statue.

Then we encountered one excuse after another.

The first was that the floor of the Rotunda might collapse under the weight of the statue. This was unconvincing, given that the statue had been in the Rotunda before. A Capitol engineer debunked excuse number one.

Then several Republican leaders invoked excuse number two: Federal dollars shouldn't be used to move the statue. Incredulous but undeterred, the Woman Suffrage Statue Campaign raised $86,000 in private donations to move the statue.

To follow up on a letter we had sent him about moving the statue, I approached Speaker Gingrich one day as he sat in the Speaker's chair. I knew he was a historian, and I appealed to his passion for history. He agreed.

It was a done deal, or so we thought. Then we heard excuse number three: The statue was too ugly. As usual, Pat Schroeder's response was the best: "Have you looked at Lincoln?"

It dawned on me that excuses number one and number three basically meant that women were being rejected for being overweight and ugly—the very same labels that do so much harm to so many American women.

The House leadership let us know that they would consider a more attractive statue of a woman. Clearly, they were missing something.

So we launched a newsletter called *The State of the Statue*. Its motto was "All the excuses that are fit to print." We published an excerpt from a *Washington Post* column by George Will: "So now we know. The answer to Freud's famous question—'What does a woman want?'—is an unattractive statue in the Capitol Rotunda" was just one of his condescending bon mots.

I responded with a letter to the editor: "Leading the battle to enfranchise half the population of the United States is no minor feat. It is one of the most significant accomplishments in our nation's history."

Finally, on Mother's Day 1997, we were successful. The statue was moved to the Rotunda. To his credit, Speaker Gingrich gave a moving speech at the dedication.

(continued on page 210)

Several countries with violent histories have voted women into power. In their campaigns, both Liberia's president, Ellen Johnson-Sirleaf, and Chile's president, Michelle Bachelet, ran on their being women, painting themselves as maternal, civilizing influences who could bring healing to countries badly in need of it.

Johnson-Sirleaf embraced the nickname "Ma Ellen" in her presidential campaign. In 2006, she delivered a speech of unusual warmth, eloquence, and grace to a joint session of Congress. She was there to thank President Bush and Congress for the extensive diplomatic efforts that helped force the former Liberian president, the dictator Charles Taylor, into exile; for an enormous $445 million appropriation that helped fund a UN peacekeeping force; and for ongoing financial support.

She spoke about how she had grown up in the Liberian countryside fishing for her dinner, eventually found her way to America, and went on to become a Harvard-educated economist, a World Bank officer, and UN assistant secretary-general. "So my feet are in two worlds," she told us, "the world of poor rural women with no respite from hardship, and the world of accomplished Liberian professionals, for whom the United States is a second and beloved home." Her country was only beginning to recover from a horrendous civil war in which young girls had been "made into sex slaves, gang-raped by men with guns, made mothers while they were still children themselves."

Her speech was a heartening reminder of the good America can do when we draw on our rich resources to export decency and human values and of the limitless opportunities our nation offers those who would give almost anything to reach our shores.

But I was touched most of all by what she said about women and girls. I was also struck by the fact that the hopes and dreams of Liberian women aren't much different from our own.

"Women, my strong constituency, tell me that they want the same chances that men have. They want to be literate. They want their work to be recognized. They want protection against rape. They want clean water that won't sicken and kill their children. We must not betray their trust."

President Bachelet of Chile has had a life equally remarkable and fraught with horror. She was imprisoned twice, tortured, and exiled during president Augusto Pinochet's regime, which also tortured and killed her father. "I was a victim of hatred, and I have dedicated my life to reversing that hatred," President Bachelet said when she was sworn in. She pledged to make her cabinet 50 percent women, to foster a more collaborative governing process, and to tackle social isues such as poverty, public health, housing, and education.

I met President Bachelet at a reception hosted by an organization called the White House Project. She offered several reasons for her election. One, she was a member of the resistance movement that had fought Pinochet. Two, she had served as Chile's defense minister, building credentials as a prospective commander in chief. Three, another woman was running for president at the same time.

The latter struck me as counterintuitive. I had always figured that two women running in a large field would split the women's vote, hurting both candidates. I later asked Marie Wilson, president of the White House Project, which works to elect more women to office in the United States, how having more than one woman candidate in a field can be helpful. She told me that when there are two women candidates, the novelty goes away, and the race ceases to be about gender. Voters stop paying attention to the candidates' hairdos and outfits and focus on what they have to say.

Today, though the statue was authorized to be in the Rotunda for only a year, it is still there. No one's about to raise the money to remove it.

Each year, thousands of schoolchildren stop to look at the suffragists, who are no longer treated as second-class revolutionaries. Every now and then, someone puts flowers at the base of the statue.

The statue is a quintessential reminder that as long as women are vastly outnumbered in legislative bodies, winning even symbolic victories for the most righteous of causes requires hard work and, yes, heavy lifting.

To help get actual funding for women's causes, occasionally you need to go even further.

Long before 9/11, along with Dana Rohrahacher (R-CA) and other colleagues, I urged the federal government to do something to address the plight of women in Afghanistan under the Taliban. The Feminist Majority Foundation sponsored events in which refugees and women's rights activists from Afghanistan told us about women and girls being killed when they went to school and being forced to live in individual prisons under the burka, a head-to-toe cloth covering that hides the face and form of the woman wearing it.

But we made little progress on the issue until America was attacked on 9/11 and Congress realized that the Taliban posed a threat to America's homeland security.

Shortly after 9/11, the Congressional Caucus on Women's Issues organized a time when members of Congress would speak on the House floor about the plight of Afghan women. I went to the floor with a burka in my hands, expecting to hold it up.

At the last minute, sensing that I needed to take drastic measures to get people focused on women in the middle of a war, I slipped the burka over my head, knowing that a picture is worth a thousand words.

It was very hard to read my speech from under a burka, which has netting in front of the eyes. Not only could I barely see, I could hardly breathe. Deciphering talking points through a burka is like reading a newspaper through a thick screen door (see page 245).

Somehow I delivered the speech, then stumbled away from the lectern, out of breath, shaken, and deeply saddened. I could only imagine what life would be like living under such an oppressive shroud.

Ten minutes later, ABC News called, followed shortly thereafter by the *New York Post.*

The speech garnered important attention in building support for the cause of assisting Afghan women. But attention is one thing; funding is another.

That battle—a multiyear, bipartisan effort with support from both women and men members—culminated in 2003. That year, I introduced an amendment calling for $60 million in aid for women-controlled programs and $5 million to fund the Afghan Independent Human Rights Commission. I tried to get the amendment to the House floor for a vote but encountered a technicality that stood in the way.

Afghan women appeared to be out of luck until the amendment was saved by another woman, Deborah Pryce, the highest-ranking Republican woman in the House. She believed passionately in the cause and tipped me off to a way to circumvent the technicality. I worked all night with the House parliamentarian to implement Deborah's suggestion and create an amendment that could get around technical barriers.

The amendment was adopted in the House, and Patty Murray (D-WA) successfully got it through the Senate. But that was no guarantee it would make it to the president's desk. The House and Senate had passed slightly different versions of the foreign appropriations bill to which the Afghan women's amendment was attached.

You have to watch these things like a hawk. They'll say yes on the House floor but then slip the language out of the bill when you're not paying attention. So when House and Senate leaders on the Appropriations Conference Committee met to reconcile differences in the overall bills, I attended the meeting, even though I wasn't on the committee and wouldn't be able to participate in the discussions.

Sure enough, they were about to strip the funding.

Fortunately, Afghan women had some strong allies in the room. Congresswoman Nita Lowey (D-NY) spoke up forcibly in favor of restoring the amendment. Then Senator Mary Landrieu (D-LA) stood up and took another drastic measure by going absolutely ballistic.

The funding survived. There's no doubt in my mind that if those women hadn't had a seat at the table, Afghan women would have been left behind.

And they still may be left behind. The fight to fund the commission is renewed in 2007. As the Taliban has reasserted itself in Afghanistan, women and girls are once again struggling to have the right to go to school, to work, to walk in public. In the last year, over 400 girls' schools and more than 40 teachers have been attacked. The Afghan Independent Human Rights Commission has proven to be an extremely valuable tool, but it will run out of funding if we don't pass new legislation this year. While we were able to get it funded in the House, as of December 2007, there was still a battle to get it through the Senate.

A CRITICAL MASS OF WOMEN

The bottom line is that we need more women in the halls of Congress and state legislatures across the country.

We are moving in the right direction. Women gained three House seats and two Senate seats in the 2006 election. Today, there are more women representatives—71—and senators—16—than ever before.

It's important because there are intrinsic differences in how men and women view the world, experience life, and set priorities. Studies from around the world have shown that gender equality furthers the causes of child survival and development.[1] In US households and abroad, women spend more money on their children's development—all while doing unpaid work.[2] These priorities show up in how women legislate. The majority of legislative ideas emanate from lawmakers' personal experiences. Inevitably, it determines how deeply one feels about an issue and how committed he or she is to it. The Women's Environment and Development Organization (WEDO) reports that "when women enter decision-making bodies in significant numbers, issues such as child care, violence against women, and unpaid labor are more likely to become priorities for policy-makers."

According to WEDO, women don't really wield power as a group in national politics until they are 30 percent of the representatives in a country's national legislature. Anything less does not give us a strong enough collective voice. Twenty-four countries have reached this "critical mass."[3] As this book went to press, 13 countries had a female head of state (which has much the same effect as having a critical mass in the legislature).

The United States, of course, didn't make the cut. Not even close.

Despite all the talk about the empowerment of American women, with just 16 percent representation in the House and Senate, we are about average.

It's a beautiful sight to see Nancy Pelosi in the Speaker's chair, fighting to stop the war, holding the Bush administration accountable for its excesses, restoring fiscal discipline to the federal budget with "pay-as-you-go" spending, and spearheading the successful effort on something I've worked hard to do: getting the 9/11 Commission Recommendations signed into law.

It's also great to see Hillary Rodham Clinton, who, as of this writing, is the first woman candidate with a serious chance of taking over the Oval Office. But it's very dangerous to look at these important role models and say, "Women have arrived in American politics. We're there." The numbers tell a different story. When it comes to political leadership, America is nowhere near being the world's most woman-friendly country.

I once heard Bella Abzug give a speech in which she said that men were screwing up the world. She went on to say that women would probably screw it up almost as badly, but we at least deserved the chance to try.

I got in the pipeline early. On the New York City Council, I was the first woman to give birth in office. In fact, I almost gave birth at the office.

I remember standing with Mayor Ed Koch at a press conference for a campaign finance reform bill we had been working on. I was more than nine months pregnant with my second daughter. Mayor Koch laughed when I said, "Campaign finance reform is long overdue, just like Baby Maloney."

After the press conference, I went inside to a City Council meeting. I started to feel funny toward the end of the debate on the floor and wondered if I was going into labor. But labor had lasted all night with my first baby, so I stayed until the meeting ended.

Virginia Marshall Maloney was born 40 minutes later at a hospital uptown. I was relieved to have made it to the hospital in time. So was my cab driver.

CALLING ALL FEMALE CANDIDATES

When I run into Marie Wilson of the White House Project, she almost always tells me to recruit more women candidates for her organization to support. So I'm going to start with you and your daughters:

Your country needs you!

Women aren't such a small minority in Congress because voters don't want to vote for women. It's because we can't win races that we don't enter. In congressional elections in 2004, male candidates outnumbered female candidates by four to one.

The shortage of congressional candidates is due in part to the lack of a strong pipeline. Candidates rarely win a seat in Congress without

No one knows more about what it takes to get into politics than Ellen Malcolm. She founded EMILY's List in 1985 to finance the campaigns of pro-choice women. EMILY stands for Early Money Is Like Yeast. Ellen was a staunch ally in my first run for reelection to Congress, when I was one of the biggest bull's-eyes for the Republican National Committee. After Hillary Clinton's 2008 primary eve rally outside Manchester, New Hampshire, I asked Ellen if she had any advice for women seeking elective public office. She told me: "Get involved with the community. Work with a group of people so that they can learn what you are capable of. Build a record of accomplishment. Then when you run, you'll have a network of people to support you and a record to run on. Too many women run for office without taking those basic steps first."

previously having served as an elected official at a lower level. But when women do run for office, they do so later in life, often waiting until long after they've started a family. So they start out behind the eight ball.

This makes it harder to break into politics, but it doesn't make it impossible. Speaker Pelosi didn't run for public office until 1987, when she was elected to Congress at age 47. Prior to that she raised five children, spending some of those years as a stay-at-home mom. Sandra Day O'Connor and Madeleine Albright were also stay-at-home moms. So it's never too late.

Nancy told me: "I found that raising a family was excellent training for public office. It forces you to focus on meeting the needs of other people, which is what I do as a legislator. But not enough women have seats at the table, and I urge more women to run."

Cindy Hall, executive director of Women's Policy, Inc., considers it essential that girls be urged from an early age to envision themselves as elected officials. Groups like EMILY's List and the Women's Campaign Forum try to send elected officials into classrooms as often as possible to encourage girls to consider public policy issues.

A WHOLE LOTTA CHUTZPAH

Whenever anyone offered me a job as a young woman, I was nothing but grateful. But if my daughter Christina is any indication, young women are moving from an era of gratitude to an era of attitude. Increasingly, they know what they want. They know they deserve it. And they're getting less and less timid about asking for it.

Christina's first job after graduating from college was as a program analyst—essentially, a researcher—for New York City Council member

In my first race for Congress, I had two opponents in the Democratic primary: an obscure attorney who wasn't a factor in the race and Abe Hirschfeld. Abe was an eccentric multimillionaire who had made a fortune building parking garages and fitness clubs. He eventually bought the New York Post, *which barely survived his tenure.*

Right after I announced my candidacy, he asked me out to lunch. It seemed like an unusual request, but I always like to size up my opponents. I had barely started to dig into my salad when Hirschfeld revealed the purpose of the meeting: he said he believed that in order to beat Republican congressman Bill Green, Democrats needed to unite behind one candidate—him. He asked me to drop out and endorse him.

I'd been serving in elected office for a decade. I had worked in public service for almost my entire career. He had been off building parking garages and fitness clubs. And he was asking me to drop out of the race!

Ladies, this is why men run the world. I don't fault Abe for asking. I admire him for it. If women had a man's sense of entitlement, we would have a real woman commander in chief instead of just a fictional one on television.

Bill de Blasio, who chaired the General Welfare Committee. It wasn't long before Christina started pushing for a more challenging role that was "closer to the action." She took a job as assistant scheduler to Council Speaker Gifford Miller. It put her at the center of activity just outside the speaker's office. A scheduler's job is not just about arranging where the boss needs to be and when. Schedulers must make political judgments about which events are more important than others. They have to artfully and diplomatically say no to important people. Schedulers also need to know everyone who is going to be in the room at an event, what issues will be discussed, and what questions their boss is likely to face. But Christina still didn't find it challenging enough, so she lobbied for a higher-ranking position as a policy analyst and got her second promotion in short order.

I hope Christina's assertiveness reflects that of the next generation. One by one, our daughters are becoming the "best man for the job." In addition to doing better in high school and making up the majority of college students, women are half of the law students and within a few years will be the majority of medical students.[4] Girls are excelling so much at school that some critics have declared that a "boy crisis" is occurring in education.

But the one way in which young women still lag behind young men may be the most important: having chutzpah. Once women's chutzpah matches their capabilities, this will no longer be a "man's world."

Nor will it, or should it, become a "woman's world." Men and boys are not the enemy. On the contrary, they are our husbands and fathers, brothers and nephews, boyfriends and "just friends," mentors and colleagues. Women's equality is not a zero-sum game. America is one country, not a nation divided between men and women. As an elected official, I ultimately can't be a partisan for one gender over another. Women's equality, not women's supremacy, is the goal.

I believe our country's best hope for solving its problems, restoring itself as a paragon of decency, and realizing the glorious vision of its founders is to recruit a new generation of women leaders—not just in Washington but also in our workplaces, congregations, communities, courts, the media, and throughout society. We need them to be committed to responsibility and accountability, to cultivate collaboration and consensus, and

One night on the House floor in the mid-1990s, Congresswoman Pat Schroeder sat down next to me and, out of the blue, asked me a philosophical question: "Carolyn, there are so many women out there struggling. How did we wind up here?"

No one had ever asked me that question, but the answer came almost right away. "My father believed in me. He told me I could do anything I wanted to do. The most important advice he ever gave me was to not learn how to type. If I did, he said, my employers would make me do nothing but type." Thirty years later, as I sat next to Pat Schroeder on the floor of the House of Representatives, I still couldn't type.

Pat smiled. "You know what?" she said. "My father told me I could do anything I wanted, too. It made a huge difference."

My father believed in me so much that when he was on his deathbed in 2000, he wrote a letter to Al Gore urging him to ask me to be his running mate.

I once asked my coauthor on this book, Bruce Corwin, why he believes so strongly in women's issues. He told me that he grew up in an egalitarian household and was inspired by his mother, Jeannette. She entered Harvard Medical School in 1954, a mere four years after her high school guidance counselor had advised that she should become a nurse because she wasn't smart enough to go to college—even though she was the class valedictorian! Jeannette's father, an orthopedist, told her that she could do anything she set her mind to and took her to his office so she could watch him treating patients.

These stories, and so many more, are vivid reminders that progress for women is everyone's responsibility. We can succeed only if fathers, mothers, and everyone else get on board.

to infuse everything they do with the decency and human values inherent in the promise of America.

Fortunately, I think our daughters are poised to reach heights that a little girl named Carolyn in Virginia Beach in the 1950s couldn't see even when she looked straight up.

With great satisfaction, I look at their propensity for service as they volunteer in their communities in record numbers.

I look at how they're at the top of the class and the bottom of a pile diving for a loose ball.

I look at their confidence and their ability to stand up for what they want and need in relationships.

I look at their resolve to forge saner, more productive workplaces; to be more involved and equal parents and more loyal friends; to foster a more a sustainable environment; to embrace people of all races, religions, ethnic backgrounds, and sexual orientations.

I marvel at their determination to be the next Mia Hamm, the next Meg Whitman, the next Oprah Winfrey, the next Mother Teresa, the next Winston Churchill, the next president of the United States.

When I look at these fantastic young females, there's only one shining conclusion I can reach:

They *are* our progress.

Take-Action Guide

A Seat at the Table

What would this country look like if Congress consisted of 16 percent *men* instead of the other way around? What if George Bush's presidency was cancelled and a real-life Mackenzie Allen (president on ABC's *Commander in Chief*) took his place? Would there be a lactation room and a child-care center at every corporation? Would credit card companies still get paid before child support in bankruptcy court? Would the United States government have so indecently decreed that the anti-torture provisions of the Geneva Conventions didn't apply to us? I have my own opinions, but there's only one way to find out.

1. Fill the pipeline.

• **Encourage your daughters to think about politics and to be active in leading their schools.** In their 2004 book *It Takes a Candidate: Why Women Don't Run for Office*, authors Jennifer L. Lawless and Richard L. Fox found that women were far less likely than men to have been encouraged by their parents to be interested in politics. Simply demonstrating interest and offering support can make an enormous difference.

• **Show and tell.** Invite local politicians, especially those who are women, to speak at your children's school or library—the younger the audience and the more often you have speakers, the better. Ask speakers to especially stress what started their interest in politics and how they began their political careers.

2. Make women's voices heard.

• **Vote!** Every time I see the statue of the suffragists in the Rotunda, I am reminded of how far we've come. Women are the single largest voting bloc in this country. We have much further to go, and the most important tool available to us all is our constitutionally guaranteed right to vote. Use it.

• **Educate yourself.** There are many voter guides available that focus on particular issues. At www.emilyslist.org, EMILY's List endorses Democratic pro-choice women candidates "from the State House all the way up to the White House."

• **Get out the vote.** Help register others to vote. EMILY's List undertakes a massive campaign you can join to help make other women a part of the democratic process.

• **Attend public meetings.** Is your neighborhood being rezoned for more commercial traffic? Is your public school system considering installing brand-name vending machines? Is there a proposal to increase the sales tax? Many of these issues are vetted at public hearings. You can be a civic leader in your community simply by doing your research and showing up for hearings on the issues that are important to you.

• **Nominate others.** Many women never enter politics because they lack encouragement or outside support. The Women's Campaign Forum lets you nominate women who could be the next generation of political leaders at www.sheshouldrun.com.

3. Run for office yourself.

• **Run for local office.** Running for a local office—these vary from community to community but can include everything from town or city council member to sheriff to school board member—can be your entrée into elected office.

• **Run for national office.** If you're ready to be a voice for a larger community, you can turn to many organizations for help. The White House Project (www.thewhitehouseproject.org) is a key player in empowering women to run for office. The Vote, Run, Lead program tackles women's leadership from all angles, from engaging the next generation to encouraging improved public perception of women candidates by endorsing positive images of women in popular culture, such as that portrayed in *Commander in Chief.* The Center for American Women and Politics (CAWP), part of Rutgers, the State University of New Jersey, is dedicated to ensuring that today's shining hopes for female leadership get a solid start. In addition to the wealth of data, research papers, and fact sheets on women in politics that it has on its Web site, it also runs a program called National Education for Women's Leadership (www.newleadership.rutgers.edu), a five-day summer course for college women designed to engage them in political life, demystify entering into politics, and plug them into a network of women leaders. CAWP also runs Ready to Run programs in several states to make politicians out of interested women. Ready to Run works in partnership with nonpartisan state-level organizations, often university women's programs. If you are interested in developing a Ready to Run program in your state, call CAWP at (732) 932-9384 or go to www.cawp.rutgers.edu/Programs/RtoRinfo.html to find out more. You can apply to have your candidacy endorsed by the Women's Campaign Forum (WCF) at www.wcfonline.org, which will endorse pro-choice female candidates of any party. Endorsed candidates are promoted heavily to the WCF membership and can also receive financial support and technical assistance. EMILY's List (www.emilyslist.org) is an immensely powerful lobbying group that specifically endorses female pro-choice candidates. It offers training and has a free downloadable guide for women interested in running for office. For qualified candidates, EMILY's List also offers technical assistance and financial support through its Political Opportunity Program.

4. Offer your talents to others.

• **Volunteer.** If you're not planning to run (or if you are thinking about it but want to get your feet wet first), there are numerous ways you can help women who are in the fray. Volunteer your time and talents to support other women in their candidacy or office. According to the Emily's List Web site, the EMILY's List Job Bank connects trainees and experienced political professionals with Democratic campaigns and progressive organizations across the country and provides support and information to Job Bank participants to help them find meaningful work and make sensible career choices. Go to www.emilyslist.org/do/jobs to find out more.

CONCLUSION

"There is a special place in hell for women who don't help other women."

—MADELEINE ALBRIGHT

My grandfather, a successful construction and real estate entrepreneur, lost everything in the Great Depression. He died of pneumonia after declaring bankruptcy.

On his deathbed, he told my grandmother to take the life insurance money, his trucks, and other equipment, and start a coal business.

My grandmother didn't have business experience or even know how to balance a checkbook. But she did have a network of friends in the Business and Professional Women (BPW) organization, which remains the nation's largest "old-girls" business network.

They spread the word that my grandmother, Christine Clegg, had six mouths to feed and encouraged everyone to heat their house with Clegg Coal. Remarkably, when it seemed that the day a woman could launch a successful industrial company might come eventually, but certainly not in the Depression, Clegg Coal became a successful start-up, operating for decades before being acquired.

My grandmother was an artist, head of the North Carolina Council of the Arts, and a great civic leader for other organizations. But BPW was always her favorite—for the sisterhood it fostered and for its support of Clegg Coal.

My grandmother was the quintessential empowered woman for her time. I wanted to be just like her. So when I asked her for career advice, I was shocked by her reply: "Get married."

I did get married, but I obviously didn't adopt her view that a woman belonged in the workforce only if a man wasn't around to provide for her. Most families today can't afford to make that choice anyway, needing two incomes to make ends meet.

Women have made great advancements since I sought my grandmother's advice, and my daughters face greater opportunities than I could have imagined at their age. Nothing exemplifies this more than the rise of two extraordinarily talented, caring, and hard-working women: House Speaker Nancy Pelosi and senator and presidential candidate Hillary Rodham Clinton.

On January 8, 2008, I traveled with my daughter Virginia to New Hampshire, hoping to see history being made in the Democratic primary. For the first time, a woman had a real shot at the Democratic nomination, although a loss in Iowa had made Hillary an underdog.

The campaign asked me to suspend for a few days my efforts to win commitments for Hillary from superdelegates (who could tip the scales at the Democratic convention in an undecided race) and head for New Hampshire to meet with women's groups—a good sign of outreach to a natural constituency that had abandoned her in Iowa. Later, we headed to Nashua, where news broadcasts continually replayed a dramatic moment. Hillary's eyes had welled up when a woman asked her how she handled the rigors of the campaign. Hillary had spoken of how the race was personal for her, not political. For a split second, she had let her guard down, and showed the country what I've seen in working with her on many issues, particularly funding health care for sick 9/11 workers, where she was particularly passionate: Hillary cares every bit as much about people as winning an election.

Later, we saw two hecklers holding "Iron My Shirt" posters disrupt a rally in Salem, angering women in the audience and reminding everyone how much gender was looming over the race.

The rally was subdued. Polls were showing her trailing Senator Barack Obama. After the rally, I had a private moment with Hillary. After she graciously signed a campaign poster for my daughter, I told her, "You're going to win." She put a brave face on but seemed downcast. "Eventually," she told me, implying that she thought she would lose New Hampshire but ultimately win the nomination.

So much for the polls. The only one with the right prediction seemed to be me. Exit polls showed that women had tipped the election in Hillary's favor. As for my grandmother decades before her, women came through when Hillary needed them most. For the first time, a woman had won a major party's state presidential primary. History had been made after all.

This book was published before the Democratic nominee had been selected. But in pursuing the presidency, Hillary faces a daunting task. People seem to love her or hate her. Surveys have shown her to be the nation's most admired woman, but many who oppose her do so with alarming vehemence. Don Imus calls her "Satan." To be sure, gender will be just one factor that decides this election. But I believe that, consciously or unconsciously, millions of men, and even some women, are threatened by a strong, outspoken woman vying for the ultimate position of power—and that's a major obstacle.

If Hillary becomes president, she will face an even more daunting challenge in pursuing equality for women, a passion of hers. The fact remains that for every Hillary Clinton, Nancy Pelosi, Oprah Winfrey, or Meg Whitman, who have broken through the glass or marble ceiling, millions of women are held back by gender bias that permeates virtually every realm of American society and global affairs.

Documenting that stark reality, as I've tried to do, is much easier than abolishing it. Raising these issues alone can be a political liability. *Crain's New York Business,* a respected business publication, once wrote a favorable article about me but qualified their praise by saying that I risked "marginalizing" myself by focusing on women's issues.

I don't believe that's an isolated view. Only an intensive, sustained chorus of activism by women and like-minded men can make these issues top priorities for *any* president. I hope you will lend your voice to the chorus.

Apathy, complacency, discouragement, and a greatly exaggerated sense of progress are the enemies of change. But we cannot stop fighting.

- Not as long as cancer patients like Linda Smith are plunged into debt until age 112 because they are underinsured.

- Not as long as blue-collar women like those Elyse advocated for face unrelenting sexual harassment that forces them out of companies that receive "Best Companies for Women" honors.

- Not as long as men can write off outings to strip clubs with clients, while families cannot write off most, if any, of their child care expenses.

- Not as long as rape victims like Michelle are denied emergency contraception prescriptions by "conscience"-ridden pharmacists who readily fill Viagra prescriptions.

- Not as long as a campaign to declare abortion murder under any circumstances is gaining steam in state legislatures and angling for a Supreme Court decision.

- Not as long as 15,000 people are trafficked into the United States, many of them women and girls, who join their American counterparts as human sex slaves for whom death is the only refuge from living hell.

- Not as long as roughly 500,000 women[1] die in childbirth every year while the US government refuses to fund UNFPA, the NGO that provides family planning and prenatal care.

- Not as long as the United States refuses to join 185 countries that are party to the Convention to End All Discrimination against Women, the only comprehensive international treaty guaranteeing women's human rights and preventing gender discrimination.

• Not as long as the 2007 Ledbetter decision stands in the Supreme Court, giving women and minorities only six months after a discriminatory incident to file a claim with the Equal Employment Opportunities Commission, even though it can take years for workers to learn know that they have been illegally discriminated against.

• And not as long as American women do not have equal rights under the Constitution.

Obviously, eventually righting these wrongs—and so many other gender-based injustices that have less to do with politics—will require long-term collective efforts by millions of women and like-minded men in our workplaces, communities, congregations, school districts, and the public square.

Pursuing leadership roles in any of these forums is a great way to make a difference. We need more women to start and lead women's networks at corporations and trade organizations. We need more women CEOs, entrepreneurs, nonprofit executive directors, justices, school board members, pastors, and coaches. And I could use *a lot* more female companionship in the US Congress.

But whatever our personal aspirations may be, we can all make progress for women, not just by writing our legislators or joining with the wonderful organizations mentioned in this book, but in our everyday lives. Each time we ask to be promoted, force an insurance company to pay a doctor's bill that it initially rejected, grill the principal on why there are twice as many teams for boys than girls at our daughters' high schools, convince a young woman to get a membership at the gym instead of a tanning salon, or tell our daughters that the sky is the limit for their futures, we make progress for all of womankind.

As my grandmother learned when she tapped a woman's network and founded Clegg Coal against all odds, and as Hillary Clinton learned in her woman-driven upset victory in New Hampshire, when women truly come together around a common cause, "eventually" can be today.

ENDNOTES

INTRODUCTION

1. See www.eeoc.gov/stats/harass.html
2. Ruy Teixeira, "Public Opinion Snapshot: Universal Health Care Momentum Swells," Center for American Progress, www.americanprogress.org/issues/2007/03/opinion_health_care.html, March 23, 2007.
3. David Leonhardt, "If Richer Isn't Happier, What Is?," *New York Times*, sec. B, May 19, 2001.
4. David Leonhardt, "A Reversal in the Index of Happy," *New York Times*, sec. C, September 26, 2007.

CHAPTER 1

1. John Dingell and Carolyn Maloney, "A New Look through the Glass Ceiling: Where Are the Women? The Status of Women in Management in Ten Selected Industries," 2002, 12.
2. US General Accounting Office, "Women's Earnings: Work Patterns Partially Explain Difference between Men's and Women's Earnings," 2003, 32.
3. Dingell and Maloney, "A New Look," 11.
4. GAO, "Women's Earnings," 5.
5. GAO, "Women's Earnings," 12.
6. Shelley Waters Boots, "The Way We Work: How Children and Their Families Fare in a 21st Century Workplace," New America Foundation, Work & Family Program, December 2004, 1.
7. Peopleclick Research Institute, "New Census Data Reveal Women's Share of Executive Positions Decreased," Peopleclick Research Institute press release, February 23, 2004.
8. Jenn Abelson, "4 Female Troopers Awarded $1M over Pregnancy Rights," *Boston Globe*, sec. B, October 5, 2002.
9. Brenda Watts was denied compensation for her claim. Department statutes required that a complaint be filed within six months of the violation; her complaint was filed at eight months.
10. The act covers workers who log more than 1,250 hours a year at workplaces having 50 or more employees within a 75-mile radius of their worksite.

11. National Coalition to Protect Family Leave, "Comments and Response to the U.S. Department of Labor's Request for Information on the Family and Medical Leave Act," statement to the United States Department of Labor, www.protectfamilyleave. org/pdf/coalition_fmla_comments.pdf, February 16, 2007, 41.

12. Kris Hundley, "The Cold Shoulder," *St. Petersburg Times*, sec. D, April 3, 2005.

13. Amy J. C. Cuddy, Susan T. Fiske, and Peter Glick, "When Professionals Become Mothers, Warmth Doesn't Cut the Ice," *Journal of Social Issues*, no. 60 (2004): 701–18.

14. Sylvia Ann Hewlett and Carolyn Buck Luce, "Off-Ramps and On-Ramps: Keeping Talented Women on the Road to Success" *Harvard Business Review*, March 2005, 52.

15. Catalyst, "Companies with More Women Board Directors Experience Higher Financial Performance, According to Latest Catalyst 'Bottom Line' Report," Catalyst press release, October 1, 2007.

16. Patricia S. Reed and Shirley M. Clark, "Win-Win Workplace Practices: Improved Organizational Results and Improved Quality of Life," research report prepared for the US Department of Labor Women's Bureau, September 2004.

17. Catalyst, "2005 Catalyst Census of Women Corporate Officers and Top Earners of the 'Fortune' 500: Executive Summary," Catalyst, 2006.

18. Ibid.

19. Jodi Grant, Taylor Hatcher, and Nirali Patel, "Expecting Better: A State-by-State Analysis of Parental Leave Programs," National Partnership for Women & Families, 2005.

20. Martin H. Malin et al. "Work/Family Conflict, Union Style: Labor Arbitrations Involving Family Care," Program on WorkLife Law, American University Washington College of Law, June 2004, 20.

21. Nancy Duff Campbell et al, "Be All That We Can Be: Lessons from the Military for Improving Our Nation's Child Care System," National Women's Law Center, April 2000.

22. Fight Crime: Invest in Kids, "Head Start Improves Achievement and Reduces Crime," Fight Crime: Invest in Kids, July 14, 2003.
    For all participants, Head Start has been shown to deliver positive near-term results in test scores, vocabulary, getting parents to read to their kids, and health, among other benchmarks. In the long term, Head Start appears to help white children a great deal—they repeat fewer grades, graduate from high school and attend college at higher rates, and have higher earnings. Early benefits for African American children are more likely to dissipate, although Head Start alumni are less likely to be involved in crime. In 2004, national standards to address variations in program quality were established, and early results have been encouraging.

23. Democratic Leadership Council, "Universal Preschool," www.dlc.org/ndol_ci.cfm?kaid=139&subid=273&contentid=253433, July 27, 2007.

24. Ibid.

25. See www.9to5/familyvaluesatwork/FV@workSummary.pdf.

26. See www.womensenews.org/article.cfm/dyn/aid/2694.

27. See www.9to5/familyvaluesatwork/FV@workSummary.pdf.

28. Linda Bray Chanow, "The Business Case for Reduced Hours," Project for Attorney Retention, Center for WorkLife Law, University of California Hastings College of the Law, www.pardc.org/Publications/business_case.shtml.

29. Malin et al., "Work/Family Conflict," 5.

30. Kimberly J. Morgan, "Child Care and the Liberal Welfare Regime: A Review Essay," *Review of Policy Research* 20, no. 4 (Winter 2003): 743–8.

31. If they have a family history of the disease and are breastfed exclusively for at least four months.

32. All statistics for breastfed chlidren are from United States Breastfeeding Committee. "Benefits of Breast Feeding." Raleigh, NC: United States Breastfeeding Committee; 2002. http://usbreastfeeding.orgiIssue-Papers/Benefits.pdf.

33. Ibid.

34. T. M. Ball and A. L. Wright. "Health Care Costs of Formula Feeding in the First Year of Life." *Pediatrics* vol. 103 no. 4, April 1999, 870–76.

35. GAO-07-817, "Women and Low-Skilled Workers: Other Countries' Policies and Practices That May Help These Workers Enter and Remain in the Labor Force," June 2007.

36. All statistics and rankings in this section, unless otherwise noted, are from the following two reports.
Jody Heymann et al. "The Work, Family, and Equity Index: Where Does the United States Stand Globally?", Project on Global Working Families, 2004.
Jody Heymann, Alison Earle, and Jeffrey Hayes, "The Work, Family, and Equity Index: How Does the United States Measure Up?", Project on Global Working Families, 2007.

37. Jacqueline H. Wolf, "Low Breastfeeding Rates and Public Health in the United States," *American Journal of Public Health* 93, no. 12 (2003): 2005.

38. Lorie Slass and Nicole Porter, "Progress or No Room at the Top? The Role of Women in Broadcast, Cable and E-Companies," Annenberg Public Policy Center, University of Pennsylvania, 2001, 2.

CHAPTER 2

1. Sarah Kershaw, "Answering the Fire Bell in the Company of Women," *New York Times*, sec. A, January 23, 2006. Only 36 of 11,430 uniformed firefighters were women.

2. Joan Williams, *Unbending Gender: Why Family and Work Conflict and What to Do about It* (New York: Oxford University Press, 2001), 29.

3. US Equal Opportunity Employment Commission, "Sexual Harassment Charges,

EEOC & FEPAs Combined: FY 1997–FY 2006," US Equal Opportunity Employment Commission, www.eeoc.gov/stats/harass.html, January 31, 2007.

4. Evelyn Murphy and E. J. Graff, *Getting Even: Why Women Don't Get Paid Like Men—And What to Do about It* (New York: Touchstone, 2005), 153.

5. Amy Joyce, "67 Women to Receive Sex-Bias Damages; Morgan Stanley to Pay $40 Million," *Washington Post*, sec. D, August 16, 2005.

6. Leonard Shapiro, "Burk-Backed Lawsuit to See $46 Million Payout," *Washington Post*, sec. E, May 3, 2007.

7. AFGE National Council of EEOC Locals, "2007 Issue Paper: Equal Employment Opportunity Commission," AFGE National Council of EEOC Locals, www.council216.org, February 20, 2007.

8. Ibid.

9. US EEOC, "Sexual Harassment."

10. Barbara A. Mikulski, "Mikulski Announces Senate Approval of EEOC Reform, Funding Increases in Spending Bill," press release, October 17, 2007.

11. Liz Pulliam Weston, "What's a Homemaker Worth? The Shocking Truth," MSN Money, http://moneycentral.msn.com/content/CollegeandFamily/P46800.asp, May 4, 2003.

12. Richard Drogin, "Statistical Analysis of Gender Patterns in Wal-Mart Workforce," prepared on behalf of plaintiff in *Dukes v. Wal-Mart Stores*, http://walmart.walmartclass.com/staticdata/reports/r2.pdf, February 2003, 11, 14.

13. Bill Pennington, "Former Top Executive at CBS Resigns from Augusta," *New York Times*, sec. D, December 3, 2002.

14. Catalyst, "Perspectives 2006: Catalyst Releases 2005 Censuses of Women Board Directors and Corporate Officers," Catalyst, August, 2006, 3.

CHAPTER 3

1. Rhea Becker, "Schroeder Recounts Tales of Congressional 'Sturm und Drang,'" *Harvard University Gazette*, www.hno.harvard.edu/gazette/1998/04.23/PatSchroederRec.html, April 23, 1998.

2. Lisa Belkin, "A Capital Idea for Women," *New York Times*, sec. G, October 4, 2007.

3. Rosemary Barnes, "Nearly 40 Percent of All Business Owners Are Women," *San Antonio Express-News*, July 16, 2005.

4. Nat Ehrlich et al., "2005 Michigan Women's Leadership Index," Inforum Center for Leadership, 2005, 5.

5. US Women's Chamber of Commerce, "About Us: National Leadership," US Women's Chamber of Commerce, www.sblink.us/html/uswcc-leaders.aspx (accessed December 13, 2007).

6. National Center for Education Statistics, "Actual and Alternative Projected Numbers for Bachelor's Degrees, by Sex of Recipient: 1988-89 to 2013-14," National

Center for Education Statistics, US Department of Education, http://nces.ed.gov/ programs/projections/projections2014/tables.asp, path: Table 27, October 2004.

7. National Science Board, "Science and Engineering Indicators 2004: U.S. S&E Labor Force Profile," National Science Board, National Science Foundation, www.nsf.gov/ statistics/seind04/c3/c3s1.htm, May 2004.

8. Donna J. Nelson, "A National Analysis of Diversity in Science and Engineering Faculties at Research Universities," University of Okalahoma, January 15, 2007 (revised October 20, 2007).

   Unless otherwise noted, statistics on women in academia are from this study.

9. Secretary of Education's Commission on Opportunity in Athletics, written testimony of Judith M. Sweet, Vice-President for the Championships/Senior Woman Administrator, National Collegiate Athletic Association, before the Secretary of Education's Commission on Opportunity in Athletics, August 27, 2002.

10. Ibid.

11. Ibid.

12. Women's Sports Foundation, "Women's Sports and Physical Activity Facts and Statistics," Women's Sports Foundation, June 15, 2007.

13. Henry Giroux, "Double Speak and the Politics of Dissent," *Dissident Voice*, www.dissidentvoice.org/Aug04/Giroux0820.htm, August 20, 2004.

14. Citizens for Tax Justice, "Year-by-Year Analysis of the Bush Tax Cuts Shows Growing Tilt to the Very Rich," Citizens for Tax Justice, www.ctj.org/html/gwb0602.htm, June 12, 2002.

15. Sharon Parrott, Edwin Park, and Robert Greenstein, "Assessing the Effects of the Budget Conference Agreement on Low-Income Families and Individuals," Center on Budget and Policy Priorities, www.cbpp.org/12-20-05bud.htm, January 9, 2006.

16. Sayer, Liana. "Gender Differences in Married Women's and Men's Responsibility for Unpaid Work," paper presented at the annual meeting of the American Sociological Association, San Francisco, August 1, 2004.

17. National Women's Law Center, "Privatizing Social Security: What's at Stake for Women," National Women's Law Center, www.nwlc.org/pdf/ WhatsAtStakeSocSec1-13-05.pdf, January 14, 2005.

18. Jeffrey R. Lewis and Cindy Hounsell, eds., "What Women Need to Know about Retirement," Heinz Family Philanthropies, 2007.

19. US Social Security Administration Office of Policy, "Annual Statistical Supplement, 2006," US Social Security Administration, June 2007.

20. Opinion Research Corporation poll, "A Nationwide Survey Shows That Americans Want a Constitutional Guarantee of Equal Rights for Women," Equal Rights Alliance, www.ratifyeraflorida.net/survey.shtml, July 2001.

CHAPTER 4

1. Sarah Arnquist, "Local Advocates for Children's Health Hope for Override of President's Veto," *Tribune*, www.sanluisobispo.com/news/local/story/161821.html, October 9, 2007.

2. David U. Himmelstein et al., "Market Watch: Illness and Injury as Contributors to Bankruptcy," *Health Affairs*, http://content.healthaffairs.org/cgi/content/full/hlthaff.w5.63/DC1, February 2, 2005.

3. Ibid.

4. Daniel Gross, "National Health Care? We're Halfway There," *New York Times*, sec. 3, December 3, 2006.

5. Himmelstein et al, "Market Watch."

6. Karen Kornbluh and Laurie Rubiner, "Leaving Women Behind," New America Foundation, www.newamerica.net/publications/articles/2004/leaving_women_behind, October 20, 2004.

7. Henry J. Kaiser Family Foundation, "Fact Sheet: Women's Health Insurance Coverage," Henry J. Kaiser Family Foundation, February 2007.

8. Henry J. Kaiser Family Foundation, "The Medicare Program: Women and Medicare," Henry J. Kaiser Family Foundation, July 2001.

9. CBS News/New York Times survey, February 2007, quoted in Ruy Teixeira, "Public Opinion Snapshot: Universal Health Care Momentum Swells," Center for American Progress, www.americanprogress.org/issues/2007/03/opinion_health_care.html, March 23, 2007.

10. James F. Fries et al., "Beyond Health Promotion: Reducing Need and Demand for Medical Care," *Health Affairs* 17, no. 2 (1998): 3.

11. World Health Organization, "Fact Sheet: Cancer," World Health Organization, www.who.int/mediacentre/factsheets/fs297/en/, February 2006.

12 American Cancer Society, "Cancer Facts and Figures 2007," American Cancer Society, 2007, 3–4.

13. Academy for Eating Disorders, "Prevalence of Eating Disorders," Academy for Eating Disorders, www.aedweb.org/eating_disorders/prevalence.cfm (accessed December 14, 2007).

14. University News Service, "Use of Diet Pills by Teen Girls Nearly Doubles," University of Minnesota, www1.umn.edu/umnnews/Feature_Stories/Use_of_diet_pills_by_teen_girls_nearly_doubles.html, November 7, 2006.

15. Sandra G. Boodman, "For More Teenage Girls, Adult Plastic Surgery," *Washington Post*, sec. A, October 26, 2004.

16. *Early Show*, "Should the Implant Ban Be Lifted?," *Early Show*, CBS News, www.cbsnews.com/stories/2005/04/12/earlyshow/health/health_news/main687545.shtml, April 12, 2005.

17. George Stamatis, "One in Three U.S. Teen Girls Use Tanning Beds," *Campus News*, Case Western Reserve University, www.case.edu/pubs/cnews/2003/9-18/tanning. htm, September 18, 2003.

18. Marit Bragelien Veierød et al., "A Prospective Study of Pigmentation, Sun Exposure, and Risk of Cutaneous Malignant Melanoma in Women," *Journal of the National Cancer Institute* 95, no. 20 (2003): 1530–38.

19. Lisa Girion,"Healthy? Insurers Don't Buy It," *Los Angeles Times*, sec. A, December 31, 2006.

20. Center on Budget and Policy Priorities, "The Number of Uninsured Americans Is at an All-Time High," Center on Budget and Policy Priorities, www.cbpp.org/ 8-29-06health.htm, August 29, 2006.

21. David Lazarus, "Health Plan Is a Private, Public Hybrid," *San Francisco Chronicle*, www.sfgate.com/cgi-bin/article.cgi?f=/c/a/2007/03/18/BUGV4OM5FC1.DTL, March 18, 2007.

22. Stephen Ohlemacher, "US Slipping in Life Expectancy Rankings," Associated Press, *Washington Post*, www.washingtonpost.com/wp-dyn/content/article/2007/08/12/ AR2007081200113.html, August 12, 2007.

23. Ibid.

24. Bureau of Labor Education, "The U.S. Health Care System: Best in the World, or Just the Most Expensive?," Bureau of Labor Education, University of Maine, Summer 2001.

25. Guy T. Saperstein, "Medicare for All: The Only Sound Solution to Our Healthcare Crisis," *AlterNet*, www.alternet.org/stories/46550, January 16, 2007.

26. Center for Responsive Politics, "Insurance: Long-Term Contribution Trends," Center for Responsive Politics, www.opensecrets.org/industries/indus.asp?Ind=F09 (accessed December 14, 2007).

27. Anthony D. Weiner, "An Ocean of Difference: New York City Seniors Pay More for Prescription Drugs than in Canada, Europe, and Japan," Special Investigations Division, Committee on Government Reform, US House of Representatives, www.house.gov/weiner/report6.htm.

28. Carolyn Maloney, "Pets and People Deserve Equal Treatment!", press release, http://maloney.house.gov/index.php?option=com_content&task=view&id=809& Itemid=61, June 1, 2000.

29. See www.nytimes.com/2007/12/15/opinion/15woolhandler.html?scp=1&sq= I+am+not+a+health+reform&st=nyt

30. Jon Kingsdale, opinion page, *Wall Street Journal*, February 7, 2007.

CHAPTER 5

1. Rape, Abuse, and Incest National Network, "Statistics," Rape, Abuse, and Incest National Network, www.rainn.org/statistics, 2006 (accessed December 17, 2007).

2. Patricia Tjaden and Nancy Thoennes, "Extent, Nature, and Consequences of Rape Victimization: Findings from the National Violence against Women Survey," National Institute of Justice, US Department of Justice, January 2006, 14.

3. Sue Orsillo, "Sexual Assault against Females," National Center for Posttraumatic Stress Disorder, US Department of Veterans Affairs, www.ncptsd.va.gov/ncmain/ncdocs/fact_shts/fs_female_sex_assault.html, May 22, 2007.

4. Kenneth S. Kendler et al., "Childhood Sexual Abuse and Adult Psychiatric and Substance Use Disorders in Women," *Archives of General Psychiatry* 57, no. 10 (2000): 953–59, as cited in New York State Coalition against Sexual Assault, "The Mental Health Impact of Sexual Trauma," New York State Coalition against Sexual Assault, www.nyscasa.org/factsheets/Mental%20Health%20Impact%20of%20Sexual%20Trauma.pdf.

5. Ibid.

6. Anthony Ramirez, "Efforts Widen to Track Down East Side Rapist," *New York Times*, sec. 13, July 6, 1997.

7. National Institute of Justice, "No Suspect Casework DNA Backlog Reduction Program," National Institute of Justice, US Department of Justice, www.ncjrs.gov/pdffiles1/nij/dnabacklog.pdf, August, 2001, 1.

8. Gerald J. Turetsky, "Take DNA When You Can," *New York Times*, Section 14, April 9, 2006.

9. Morgan Quinto Press, "13th Annual America's Safest (and Most Dangerous) Cities," Morgan Quinto Press, www.morganquinto.com/cit07pop.htm, 2007.

10. Julia Preston, "For '73 Rape Victim, DNA Revives Horror, Too," *New York Times*, sec. A, November 3, 2005.

11. Rape, Abuse, and Incest National Network, "Statistics."

12. Julia Preston, "Man Sentenced for 1973 Rape; Victim Berates 'Rabid Beast,'" *New York Times*, sec. B, November 29, 2005.

13. Rape, Abuse, and Incest National Network, "Statistics."

14. Ibid.

15. Matthew R. Durose and Patrick A. Langan, "Felony Sentences in State Courts, 2000," Bureau of Justice Statistics, US Department of Justice, June 2003.

16. Rape, Abuse, and Incest National Network, "Punishing Rapists," Rape, Abuse, and Incest National Network, www.rainn.org/statistics/punishing-rapists.html, 2006 (accessed December 17, 2007).

17. Kelley Beaucar Vlahos, "Kobe Case Draws Attention to Athlete Allegations," FoxNews, www.foxnews.com/story/0,2933,103248,00.html, November 17, 2003.

18. Bureau of Justice Statistics, "Intimate Partner Violence in the U.S.: Injury and Treatment," Bureau of Justice Statistics, US Department of Justice, www.ojp.usdoj.gov/bjs/intimate/injury.htm, December 28, 2006.

19. Cathy Young, "Domestic Violence: An In-Depth Analysis," Independent Women's Forum, www.iwf.org/news/show/19011.html, September 30, 2005.

20. Patsy Klaus, "Crime and the Nation's Households, 2004," Bureau of Justice Statistics, US Department of Justice, April 2006.

21. Office of Justice Programs, "Intimate Partner Violence Declined between 1993 and 2004," Office of Justice Programs press release, US Department of Justice, www.ojp.usdoj.gov/newsroom/2006/BJS07007.htm, December 28, 2006.

22. Ibid.

23. Ibid.

24. Family Violence Prevention Fund, "Domestic Violence Is a Serious, Widespread Social Problem in America: The Facts," Family Violence Prevention Fund, www.endabuse.org/resources/facts, 2007 (accessed December 17, 2007).

25. US General Accounting Office, "Domestic Violence: Prevalence and Implications for Employment among Welfare Recipients," US General Accounting Office, November 1998, 8.

26. Katharine Zambon, "Huge Shelter Shortage for Domestic Violence Victims," *Street Sense*, www.streetsense.org/articles/article_0706violence.jsp, July 2006.

27. Ibid.

28. Family Violence Prevention Fund, "One in Five Teenage Girls Experiences Dating Violence," Family Violence Prevention Fund, http://endabuse.org/newsflash/index.php3?Search=Article&NewsFlashID=269, August 2, 2001.

CHAPTER 6

1. Donna Abu-Nasr, "Organized 'Sex Tour' Industry Growing in U.S.," Associated Press, Washington Dateline, March 16, 1998.

2. Helen Peterson, "DA Says He Can't Move vs. Sex Tour Operator," *Daily News* (New York), sec. A, January 5, 2000.

3. David Masci, "Human Trafficking and Slavery," *CQ Researcher* 14, no. 12 (March 2004): 276, 280.

4. The snack bar where Nuch experienced forced prostitution was not a destination for Big Apple clients. To read more about Nuch and other victims of trafficking, see Human Rights Watch's special report at www.hrw.org/reports/2000/japan/4-profiles.htm.

5. US Department of State, "Release of the Seventh Annual Trafficking in Persons Report," US Department of State, www.state.gov/g/tip/rls/rm/07/86306.htm, June 12, 2007.

6. Mark Jacobson, "The $2,000-an-Hour Woman," *New York* magazine, http://nymag.com/nymetro/nightlife/sex/features/12193, July 10, 2005.

7. Bridging Refugee Youth and Children's Services, "Child Trafficking: Serving Survivors, Sharing Resources," Bridging Refugee Youth and Children's Services, US Conference of Catholic Bishops/Migration and Refugee Services, www.brycs.org/ChildTrafficking.htm, 2006 (accessed December 17, 2007).

8. Office of Safe and Drug-Free Schools, "Human Trafficking of Children in the United States," Office of Safe and Drug-Free Schools, US Department of Education, www.ed.gov/about/offices/list/osdfs/factsheet.html, June 26, 2007 (accessed December 17, 2007).

9. Rugh Parriott, "Health Experiences of Twin Cities Women Used in Prostitution: Survey Findings and Recommendations," unpublished, May 1994.

10. Melissa Farley, "Prostitution and Trafficking in Nine Countries: An Update on Violence and Posttraumatic Stress Disorder," *Journal of Trauma Practice* 2, no. 3/4 (2004): 33–74.

11. Janice G. Raymond, "Health Effects of Prostitution," Coalition against Trafficking in Women, www.uri.edu/artsci/wms/hughes/mhvhealt.htm, February 1999.

12. John J. Potterat, "Mortality in a Long-term Open Cohort of Prostitute Women," *American Journal of Epidemiology* 159, no. 8 (2004): 778–85.

CHAPTER 7

1. Les Kinsolving, "Contraception, Mr. President—For or Against?," WorldNetDaily, www.worldnetdaily.com/news/article.asp?ARTICLE_ID=45296, July 16, 2005.

2. See my timeline at http://maloney.house.gov/index.php?option=content& task=view&id=1134&Itemid=61.

3. National Campaign to Prevent Teen Pregnancy, "Teen Sexual Activity in the United States," National Campaign to Prevent Teen Pregnancy, www.teenpregnancy.org/ resources/data/pdf/TeenSexActivityOnePagerJune06.pdf, June 2006.

4. Henry J. Kaiser Family Foundation, "U.S. Teen Sexual Activity," Henry J. Kaiser Family Foundation, www.kff.org/youthhivstds/upload/ U-S-Teen-Sexual-Activity-Fact-Sheet.pdf, January 2005.

5. Katherine Suellentrop and Christine Flanigan, "Science Says: Pregnancy among Sexually Experienced Teens," National Campaign to Prevent Teen Pregnancy, April 2006, cited in Planned Parenthood, "Pregnancy & Childbearing Among U.S. Teens," Planned Parenthood, www.plannedparenthood.org/files/PPFA/fact-teen-pregnancy.pdf, September 2007, 1–2.

6. Lawrence B. Finer and Stanley K. Henshaw, "Disparities in Rates of Unintended Pregnancy in the United States, 1994 and 2001," *Perspectives on Sexual and Repro-ductive Health* 38, no. 2 (2006) 90–6, cited in Planned Parenthood, "Pregnancy & Childbearing among U.S. Teens," Planned Parenthood, www.plannedparenthood. org/files/PPFA/fact-teen-pregnancy.pdf, September 2007, 2.

7. Tamara Kreinin, "The Framing of a Debate: 10 Years of the Abstinence-Only-Until-Marriage Message," SIECUS Report, www.siecus.org/pubs/srpt/srpt0046.html, 2004.

8. Committee on Government Reform, "The Content of Federally Funded Abstinence-Only Education Programs," Committee on Government Reform, US House of Representatives, www.democrats.reform.house.gov/ Documents/20041201102153-50247.pdf, 12.

9. Committee on Gov. Reform, "Abstinence-Only Education Programs," 24–25

10. Committee on Gov. Reform, "Abstinence-Only Education Programs," 26.

11. Planned Parenthood, "HPV," Planned Parenthood, www.plannedparenthood.org/ sexual-health/std/hpv.htm, June 28, 2007 (accessed December 17, 2007).

12. Janet Guyon, "The Coming Storm over a Cancer Vaccine," *Fortune*, http://money. cnn.com/magazines/fortune/fortune_archive/2005/10/31/8359188/index.htm, October 31, 2005.

13. Françoise Girard, "Global Implications of U.S. Domestic and International Policies on Sexuality," *Sexual Policy Watch*, Working Papers, no. 1, June 2004, 7.

14. Committee on Gov. Reform, "Abstinence-Only Education Programs," 11.

15. Alba DiCenso et al., "Interventions to Reduce Unintended Pregnancies among Adolescents: Systematic Review of Randomised Controlled Trials," BMJ, www.bmj. com/cgi/content/full/324/7351/1426#F5, June 15, 2002.

16. John S. Santelli et al., "Explaining Recent Declines in Adolescent Pregnancy in the United States: The Contribution of Abstinence and Improved Contraceptive Use," *American Journal of Public Health* 97, no. 1 (2007): 1–7.

17. Committee on Gov. Reform, "Abstinence-Only Education Programs," 1.

18. Laura McPhee, "The Conscience Clause," www.nuvo.net, May 4, 2005.

19. Ibid.

20. US Government Accountability Office, "Decision Process to Deny Initial Application for Over-the-Counter Marketing of the Emergency Contraceptive Drug Plan B was Unusual," US Government Accountability Office, November 2005, 21.

21. Planned Parenthood, "Emergency Contraception: Effectiveness," Planned Parenthood, www.plannedparenthood.org/birth-control-pregnancy/ emergency-contraception/effectiveness-4368.htm, 2007 (accessed December 17, 2007).

22. Ibid.

23. Anna Glasier and David Baird, "The Effects of Self-Administering Emergency Contraception," *New England Journal of Medicine* 339, no. 1 (1998): 1–4, and P. Van Look and F. Stewart, "Emergency Contraception," in R. A. Hatcher et al., eds., *Contraception Technology*, 17th ed. (New York: Ardent Media, 1998).

24. National Abortion Federation, "Crisis Pregnancy Centers: An Affront to Choice," National Abortion Federation, www.prochoice.org/pubs_research/publications/ downloads/public_policy/cpc_report.pdf, 2006.

25. National Abortion Federation, "Crisis Pregnancy Centers," 12.

26. National Abortion Federation, "Crisis Pregnancy Centers," 7.

27. Planned Parenthood, "Who Is Eric Keroack?" Planned Parenthood, www.plannedparenthood.org/news-articles-press/politics-policy-issues/medical-sexual-health/keroack-11092.htm, December 15, 2006.

28. Amanda Schaffer, "The Family Un-Planner," Slate, www.slate.com/id/2154249, November 21, 2006.

29. Jacqueline Forrest and Renée Samara, "Impact of Publicly Funded Contraceptive Services on Unintended Pregnancies and Implications for Medicaid Expenditures," *Family Planning Perspectives* 28, no. 4 (1996): 188–95, cited in Planned Parenthood, "America's Family Planning Program: Title X," www.plannedparenthood.org/news-articles-press/politics-policy-issues/birth-control-access-prevention/family-planning-6553.htm, June 6, 2007.

30. CNN, "Supreme Court Strikes down Controversial Nebraska Abortion Law," CNN, http://archives.cnn.com/2000/LAW/06/28/scotus.partialbirth/index.html, June 28, 2000.

31. JUSTICE KENNEDY: Suppose—this might help—suppose the physician testifies that "I wanted to do a nonintact, an in utero D&E, that, that's, that was my intent, that's what I wanted to do, that's what I always want to do. In this case I had an intact delivery and had no other choice." Are you saying that we could interpret the statute to say that that is not the prohibited criminal intent, he is immune from prosecution in that case?

32. See my scorecard online at http://maloney.house.gov/documents/reproductivechoice/choicescorecard/Choice_Scorecard.pdf.

33. Human Rights Watch, "Owed Justice: Thai Women Trafficked into Debt Bondage in Japan," www.hrw.org/reports/2000/Japan, September 2000.

34. Indrias Getachew, "Early Marriage and Girls' Education in Ethiopia: An Interview with Tenagnework Anegagre," UNICEF, www.unicef.org/teachers/forum/1002.htm, October 2002.

35. UNICEF, "Changing a Harmful Social Convention: Female Genital Mutilation/Cutting," UNICEF, www.unicef-irc.org/publications/pdf/fgm-gb-2005.pdf, 2005, 1.

36. Department of Reproductive Health and Research, "Maternal Mortality in 2000: Estimates Developed by WHO, UNICEF, and UNFPA," Department of Reproductive Health and Research, World Health Organization, 2004, 17.

37. UNFPA news release, July 22, 2002.

38. Christian Coalition of America, "Washington Weekly Review," Christian Coalition of America, www.cc.org/content.cfm?id=230, June 17, 2005.

39. Larry Nowels and Connie Veillette, "International Population Assistance and Family Planning Programs: Issues for Congress," Congress Research Service, Library of Congress, June 6, 2006.

40. David Prentis, "The Contracepted Society," Population Research Institute, www.pop.org/main.cfm?id=94&r1=1.00&r2=1.00&r3=0&r4=0&level=2&eid=873 (accessed December 17, 2007).

41. Betsy Illingworth, "The Global Gag Rule," Planned Parenthood, www.plannedparenthood.org/news-articles-press/politics-policy-issues/international-issues/gag-rule-13105.htm, January 2, 2006.

42. UNFPA news release, July 22, 2002.

43. University of Southhampton, UK, End of Project Survey, UNFPA program in China. www.s3ri.soton.ac.uk/projects/proj_unfpa.php

44. National Abortion Federation, "Crisis Pregnancy Centers," 13.

CHAPTER 8

1. Elizabeth M. King and Andrew D. Mason, "Engendering Development Through Gender Equality in Rights, Resources, and Voice," World Bank and Oxford University Press, January 2001.

2. Franz Brotzen, "Economist Backs Recommitment to World Development Goals," Rice University, www.media.rice.edu/media/NewsBot.asp?MODE=VIEW&ID=10207, November 2, 2007.

3. Women's Environment and Development Organization, "Getting the Balance Right in National Cabinets," Women's Environment and Development Organization, www.wedo.org/files/women%20in%20cabinets2007.pdf, 2007, 1.

4. Princeton Review, "Where My Girls At?", Princeton Review, www.princetonreview.com/law/research/articles/decide/gender.asp (accessed December 17, 2007), and Dean Deborah Powell, "State of the Medical School 2004: A Focus on the Future," University of Minnesota, www.med.umn.edu/about/stateof04/home.html, November 15, 2004.

CONCLUSION

1. World Health Organization, www.who.int/research/en/

In 1992, the "Year of the Woman," it was thrilling to see 26 new women walk down the aisle—not to get married, but to be sworn into the US Congress. Here I am being at the ceremonial swearing-in with my daughters, Christina and Virginia. *(Photo courtesy of the author)*

Post 9/11, the federal government proposed giving larger settlements to men who made the same salaries as women based on lifetime earnings expectancy. Working with Legal Momentum, we got the government to nix the proposal that would have institutionalized the wage gap. I am pictured here with a construction worker on 9/12 at Ground Zero. *(Photo courtesy of the author)*

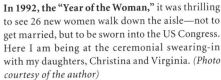

On the eve of her stunning victory in New Hampshire, Hillary Clinton signed campaign posters for Congresswoman Sheila Jackson-Lee (D-TX) and me. Defying the polls and the pundits who wrote her off after Iowa, women voters turned out in massive numbers to ensure that rumors of the demise of her campaign had been greatly exaggerated. *(Photo © Dan Videtich)*

Women played a big role in passing the ban on assault weapons. Urged on by the NRA, the Republican Congress allowed the ban to expire, abandoning any semblance of a sane gun control policy to protect women, children, and families. *(Photo courtesy of the author)*

In 2004, 750,000 women, men, and children staged the largest-ever march on Washington—the March for Women's Lives—to protect the right to choose. Christina and Virginia joined me at the march *(left)*. *(Photo courtesy of the author)*

Here I am marching with *(left to right)* president of NARAL Kate Michaelman, president of Planned Parenthood Gloria Feldt, former Secretary of State Madeleine Albright, me, Rep. Sheila Jackson-Lee (D-TX), Rep. Louise Slaughter (D-NY), and Speaker Nancy Pelosi (D-CA). *(Photo courtesy of the author)*

With Martha Burk *(above)* of the National Council of Women's Organizations and others protesting discrimination at the all-male Augusta National Golf Club. I've introduced legislation to ban tax breaks for business expenses incurred at clubs that discriminate on the basis of sex. *(Photo © AP Images/Roberto Borea)*

In 2001, I gave a House-floor speech in a burka *(right)*, the oppressive garb that the Taliban force many Afghan women to wear. We ultimately garnered $60 million in financial aid and funded a new Human Rights Commission.

I celebrated the issuance of a US postal stamp honoring the Women's Rights Movement in 2001 with some great women leaders. Pictured are *(left to right)* Ellie Smeal, Geraldine Ferraro, Lucille Hartman, Anna Kril, Anne Bruno, Mim Kelber, Kathy Bonk, Vinnie Malloy, me, Barbara Seaman, Susan Brownmiller, Gloria Steinem, and Liz Holtzman. *(Photo courtesy of the author)*

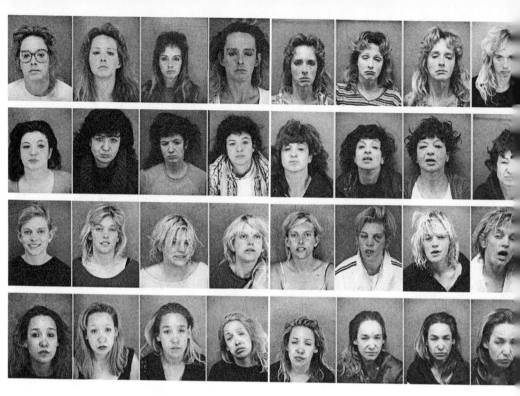

Depictions of prostitution in the media and popular culture (including the movie *Pretty Woman*) can be grossly misleading, even glamorous. In fact, street prostitutes are typically trafficked, exploited, battered, and often force-fed drugs by slavemaster pimps. This series of mugshots of street prostitutes, which documents their first arrest to their eighth, illustrates the reality of life on the street, which more closely resembles a descent into hell than a Hollywood movie.

INDEX

★ ★ ★

Underscored page references indicate boxed text.